The Manual
Vol. 4

Central Virginia Sport Performance

The fourth collaboration of works from our contributors

The Manual
Vol. 4

Central Virginia Sport Performance

Edited By:
Jay DeMayo, CSCS
Andrew White, MS, CSCS
Mike Thomson, MS, CSCS
Mike Dahlem, M Ed.

Published by: Central Virginia Sport Performance,
Richmond VA 23238
For information and to order copies: www.cvasps.com

Contents

Forward ix

Chapter 1: Operationalizing Excellence: The Performance C.O.D.E.
by Teena Murray 1

    Culture (C) 3

    Culture Summary 6

    Operating System (O) 6

    Aligning Processes 7

    Organizing People 8

    Data & Decisions (D) 9

    Execution (E) 11

    Summary 14

Chapter 2: Differences Between Tactical and Collegiate Strength and Conditioning
by Andrew White MS, CSCS 19

    The Athlete 20

    The Training 23

    The Realities 31

    Conclusion 34

Chapter 3: The Performance Director's Secret Soft Syllabus
by Fergus Connolly 37

    Communication – an Introduction 38

    Why we communicate 39

    Learning from Others 40

    Intrapersonal Communication 41

    The Communication Process 41

    Audience Perspective 42

    Feedback 44

    Message 45

    Delivery 46

Reinforcement..46

Barriers to Effective Communication 47

Keys to Effective Communication 47

Additional Thoughts...48

Communication Skills 48

Conclusion..50

Chapter 4: Mental Resilience Training
by Dan A. Pfaff 53

Module 1: Teaching Resilience to Athletes..57

Module 2: Elite Athlete Development, Building Mental Toughness 57

Module 3: Elite Athlete Experiences, Explanatory
Styles and Thinking Traps 58

Module 4: Going Deeper; Icebergs or Deeply Held Beliefs 59

Module 5: The Battery System for Development, Energy Management............59

Problem Solving 60

Fighting Back Against Counterproductive Thoughts in "REAL TIME" 61

Cultivating Gratitude..62

Identifying Character Strengths 62

Strengthening Relationships 63

Sustaining Mental Resiliency...64

Enhanced MRT Components 65

Chapter 5: Summation of Force
by Jeff Moyer and Brian Mathews 69

Summation of Forces:...71

Muscles and Sequence of Actions:..72

Practical: 75

Chapter 6: Culture Club: A Story of Struggle and Growth in High Performance Sport
by Devan McConnell 81

Culture..83

Accountability..85

Trust..85

Touch..86

Communication. 86
Leadership. 86
Unifying Vision. 87
Connection. 87
A Framework for Culture 88
Transparency 88
Player Involved Discussion 89
Player Directed Accountability 91
Developing Trust 93
Touch 96
Communication 96
Leadership Education 97
Vision 99
Pay The Man. 100
The History of the Program 101
About that Why 104

Chapter 7: The Team Behind the Team
by Keenan Robinson 109
The Physician 110
The Athletic Trainer 113
The Chiropractor 115
The Sport Physiologist/ Sports Scientist 117

Chapter 8: Boring Stuff That Works
by Andrew Althoff 121
Layer 1 – Philosophical Simplicity 122
Layer 2 – Assessing Progress and Measuring Success 124
Layer 3 – Performance Development 126
Layer 4 – Defining The Buckets 128
Layer 5 – Creating A Cultural Identity 134
Layer 6 – Implementing The Cultural Plan 135
Layer 7 – Assessing The Culture 137
Summary 138

Chapter 9: Sport Science Data Infrastructure
by Landon Evans 141
- Why listen to me? 142
- Chapter scope 143
- Technical Jargon 143
- Why Consider Infrastructure Design? 144
- Where to start? 144
- Data Acquisition 146
- Standard operating procedures 146
- Service Testing of Hardware 147
- Data Post Processing 147
- Extract 147
- Transform 150
- Load 151
- Data Storage 152
- Data Modeling and Visualization 153
- Interactive Querying 153
- Visualization 154
- Data Publishing 156
- Athlete Management Systems vs Make Your Own 156
- Our Infrastructure 157
- Conclusion 158

Chapter 10: Sleep and Adaptation
by Dr. Erik Korem 161
Preface 162
- Training – An Adaptive Process 170
- DC Potential and the Training Process 176
- The Connection 177
- Coaching Points 178
- References 180

Forward

Understanding to take care of those who are working behind the scenes is something that I've discussed a bit in the past. In the 57th My Thoughts Monday I discuss taking care of those that sit by you, meaning your walk-ons and red shirts, during the season. Similar to these unsung heroes who put in tons of time with little to no reward, the other people who sit by the strength coach on the bench deserve some notoriety and support as well. Despite the fact that some coaches have better seats on their bench then I do, I would wager that if you're having success with the program, these two people are right there fighting the good fight with you.

The sports medicine professional, commonly referred to as your athletic trainer, can be a strength coaches' best friend or worst nightmare. Not only is mine one of my best friends, he is, in my opinion, the unicorn. He's a person who has had not just the highest level of support of the weight room, but also every other aspect of "high performance". He has pushed for more monitoring, deeper evaluation for recovery, and improving how we fuel our student athletes. As you read through the following pages you will find multiple people discussing communication, relationships, and collaborations with sports med. Due to his superior skillset, and understanding of what our goals and principles are as a performance department, he has been our leader and drives us forward.

The academic coordinator is probably the most over looked, but probably most important. If the athletes aren't eligible I don't care if they're hurt or crushing it in the weight room. This man has been a mentor, a leader, and someone who has constantly kept me in check, even when I didn't think I needed it. He got more out of our student athletes by simply getting out of their way and making them be accountable to their responsibilities. Due to this, the little things, and the details were never an issue.

Those two men that have been at the end of the bench with will  never know how much of an impact they've had on me, and how much better of a coach and person they've made me. For that, King and A-Train, I can't thank you enough. Here's to you guys, because without you two asking me to be better each day, I can say without hesitation that this would not have been possible. Thanks for pushing me through the the follies and picking up when I was almost falling over.

1

Operationalizing Excellence: The Performance C.O.D.E.

Teena Murray

Sr. Director of Athlete Health & Performance

Sacramento Kings

In 2009, *Simon Sinek* told us to *Start with WHY* to be better leaders, create more inspired followers, and, generally be more successful at whatever it is we do. I agree. A clear purpose (hopefully driven by our passion) is always a critical first step. I would suggest, however, that as teachers, coaches and mentors, knowing our *WHY* and leading with it, is not a new (or challenging) notion. In fact, some of us may lean too heavily on our *WHY*, and may not spend enough time thinking about, developing, aligning and executing our *HOW*. I believe this is where we **operationalize excellence** and create our unique competitive advantage.

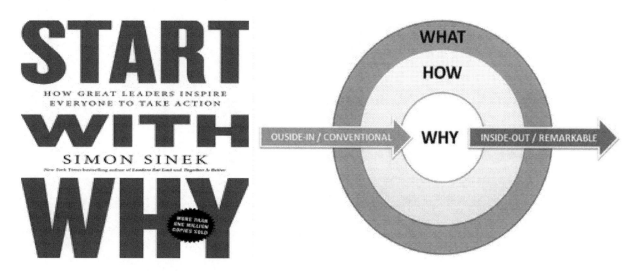

Figure 1. Simon Sinek's Start With WHY

HOW organizations (and people inside organizations) do what they do has always fascinated me. Whether it's reading a mission statement on the wall of a small business, or a quote on the wall of a college weight room, I want to know *WHY* it's there, but more so, *HOW* it influences and organizes the people and the work being done. Does it?

As with many of you, I have studied the inner workings of great companies such as Google, Disney, Pixar, Hewlett-Packard, and Toyota, and I have read much from the social sciences, and business and leadership literature on the topics of culture, human behavior, organizational dynamics, and strategy deployment.

What I know for sure (to steal Oprah's words) is there is power in *HOW*. Take Pixar, for example. Their *'secret sauce'* is absolutely their *HOW*. From *HOW* they put the wellbeing of their people first, to *HOW* they intentionally focus on uniting around a shared purpose (making great films), *HOW* they encourage diversity and self-expression, *HOW* they design their office spaces to promote community and interaction, and *HOW* they structure constructive feedback mechanisms ("Brain trusts"), their leaders are intentional about all of it.

In our turbulent and fast-paced world of sport, HOW we simplify the complex is everything. *HOW* we identify and recruit talent, *HOW* we organize people and processes, *HOW* we manage and integrate data, and most importantly, *HOW* we communicate and execute, is critical for achieving sustained success.

In this chapter I will present a conceptual framework for defining, developing, aligning, and executing your *HOW*. Regardless of whether you're a performance coach working with a single team, or a performance director leading an entire program, the template is relevant.

The framework- which I call the **Performance C.O.D.E.**- has evolved during my over two decades in the field as a Performance Coach and Performance Director. It has been shaped by a variety of readings and experiences and refined by my former staff at the University of Louisville, where we built our Sports Performance program around the 4 pillars that define the **Performance C.O.D.E.**- Culture, Operating System, Data & Decisions and, Execution.

Culture (C)

"The true evidence of culture is how people behave when no one is watching."
-Anonymous

The first, and arguably most important, pillar of the **Performance C.O.D.E.** framework, is Culture (C). Whether we realize it or not, culture is always on display. It's the "smell of the place" represented by the attitudes and behaviors of everyone involved. I believe culture is simply *'what it means to be (and feels like to be) one of us.'* If the people on your team don't know what it means to be there, wearing the logo, then you have no culture.

In 2014, culture was Merriam Webster's word of the year. It has become a prolific buzz word in sport: overused, misrepresented, and oftentimes misunderstood. By definition it is a commitment to shared attitudes, norms, values, behaviors, traditions, and symbols.

The 8-year *Stanford Project on Emerging Companies* (SPEC) arrived at a similar conclusion after studying over 200 high-tech startups in Silicon Valley. Authors Baron & Hannan (2002) found that the companies that endured and prospered during very difficult times (the dot-com explosion) were the ones where founders disproportionately chose a commitment model of development, prioritizing values and relationships, and recruiting according to cultural fit over 'star' talent.

In *Built to Last*, Jim Collins examined 18 exceptional companies that have stood the test of time. A core ideology- core values and a sense of purpose beyond just making money guided 17 of those 18. They didn't simply trust in good intentions or values statements, rather they created a 'cult-like culture' that became deeply rooted in all aspects of the business.

One of the best examples of a culture in sport has to be the famous rugby All-Blacks of New Zealand- the all-time most successful international sport organization. One of my favorite books, *Legacy*, shares the 15 principles that form the constitution by which that team lives, including *'leave the jersey better than you found it.'* These principles shape the behaviors (i.e.: *'sweep the sheds)'* and traditions (i.e.: *pre-game Haka*) that define what it means to be one of them.

During my time at the University of Louisville, we also attempted to be 'cult-like' in developing and sustaining our culture- both within the 22 teams with whom we worked, and within our own team– the Louisville Sports Performance Team. We wrote our mission on the wall, and we built everything else around it.

'Build Athletes, Prepare Champions' and, do it as a team. That's it. That's all we needed. Over my 14 years leading the program, every time we hired- whether a new full-time coach, or a Summer intern- we vetted candidates on alignment to our purpose and our values above all. We were team-centric, sharing responsibility for every aspect of our operation. We had clear values, and we held each other accountable. We understood

that the program and our athletes always came first, and it was our goal to leave both *'better than we found it.'*

Figure 2. The Purpose Wall

A few examples of *HOW* we lived our culture include: wearing the same color shirts each day of the week, sharing updates and priorities for the week in our 'Five-Bullet Monday' staff meetings (all credit to Tim Ferriss), working out together on Friday mornings (tradition), sharing our quarterly goals on the bulletin board in our conference room (team support and accountability), and participating in our annual staff hockey game (tradition).

Across the 22 teams we served, we implemented our **CARDINAL CODE** to create a common language, drive competition, and shape our environment. Step #3, "Finish Strong" involved a simple challenge or competition (for the entire group, or selected individuals) at the end of team workouts that had to be successfully completed or 'won'. This often led to loud unifying events in our 12,000 square foot facility, sometimes with our entire coaching staff on the floor cheering the team(s) of the hour.

Figure 3. CARDINAL CODE

Culture Summary

Your culture should align with your mission or purpose (WHY) and should determine WHO you recruit to be a part of your team, HOW you structure your environment, and HOW you craft your strategy.

Operating System (O)

The second pillar of the **Performance C.O.D.E.** is a solid *Operating System* (O) to organize people and align processes. It should be designed from a clear philosophy and set of training principles, and designed to create a common language, and pathway to lasting performance. Most importantly, it should align with your *WHY*.

Creating a powerful *Operating System* begins with identifying clear target outcomes (2-4) and associated key performance indicators (KPI's). KPI's are the specific measurables that demonstrate how effectively you are achieving your outcomes. As performance coaches/directors, our target outcomes usually revolve around injury prevention and performance enhancement, without objective KPI's to support our impact on both.

Figure 4. Operating System Checklist

Unfortunately, unlike the business world, KPI's in sport are often an afterthought. They aren't debated or discussed until there's a setback, losing streak, or 'less-than' season. Being clear about your KPI's at the outset, and sharing responsibility for them, allows for more focused planning, execution, evaluation, and improvement.

At Louisville, our target outcomes were: 1) minimize risk of non-contact injury, 2) maximize athlete development (using our LTAD model), and, 3) optimize team success. Our associated KPI's were: a) # of games missed due to non-contact injury per season b) % change (during the off-season) in key performance qualities/capacities, and c) team post-season winning percentage.

Aligning Processes

As you might remember, at Louisville our mission was *"Build Athletes, Prepare Champions"*, and do it as a team (a multidisciplinary high-performance team). Our *Operating System* was developed accordingly- target outcomes, philosophy, and methodology designed with *the mission* in mind.

Our philosophy and training principles centered around being holistic, athlete-centered, assessment-based, evidence-focused and coach-driven, and our methodology (accordingly) started with our Cardinal High-Performance Assessment. The assessment- which included screening, testing, and tracking components- unified our performance team (sports medicine, sports nutrition, sport psychology, and strength and conditioning), led to the creation of a universal language, and the development of our risk, readiness, return-to-performance, and athlete development processes.

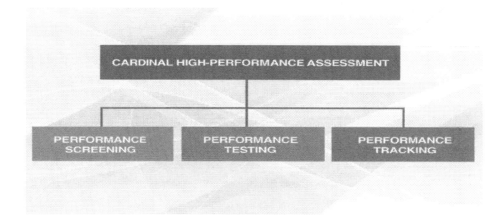

Figure 5. High-Performance Assessment (3 prongs)

Organizing People

Without question, the greatest challenge with moving toward a progressive, high-performance approach is organizing people. Change is hard, period. Whether it's changing mindset to change attitudes and behaviors or changing structures (eliminating silos) to change function (collaboration), it's not easy.

Given our desire for high-performance at Louisville, it was essential to employ a flat and agile organizational structure. After all, high-performance by definition is agile and team-centric, with work organized around whole processes, not narrow job titles and functions. An outdated (top-down) command and control structure, in which decision-making was centralized to one leader (me), was not the answer. We also wanted our structure to optimize the wingspan of our resources and expertise, encourage autonomy and creativity, and support the growth and development of our practitioners. After all, keeping our talent in the building (in our program) was second only to getting the talent in the building in the first place!

When *Team of Teams* came along in 2015 we were already (organically) organizing into small teams around specific needs, and content areas, and empowering "leaders" within our staff according to their core expertise, but General McChrystal's book (a gift from a friend) took our structure (and ultimately our function) to a new level.

We soon adopted a *Team of Teams* approach, creating diverse teams of 3-5 people (from across the health and performance disciplines) to manage key areas of our operation. They were charged with studying the literature, following the "experts" and watching the trends to ensure that our methods and protocols were best-in-class. They were also encouraged to be innovative, to try new things, investigate R&D possibilities (especially on our campus), and lead curriculum development within our mentorship program. Our *Team of Teams* structure grew each year to eventually include eight areas- Recovery, Analytics, Strength & Power, Mentorship, Bioenergetics, Speed, Assessment, and Return-to-Performance- and representation from medical, nutrition, psychology, mental health, leadership and strength and conditioning.

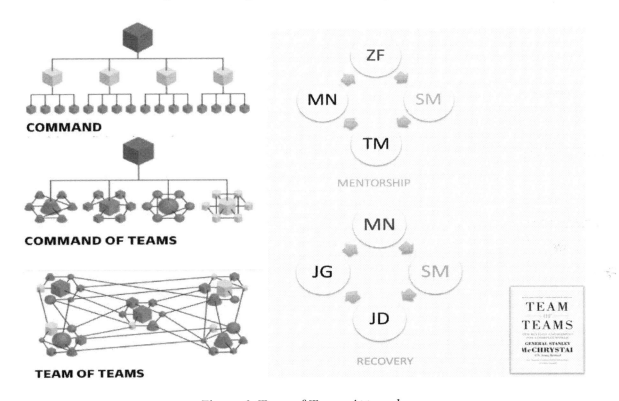

Figure 6. Team of Teams Approach

Data & Decisions (D)

The third pillar of the **Performance C.O.D.E.** framework is Data & Decisions (D). This pillar should be integrated, if not interwoven, into your *Operating System*, but comes AFTER you have constructed your methodology- and know where data will enhance your processes (or at least have some pretty good ideas).

As an *'early adopter'*, it's easy to spend time being overwhelmed by data, and what we don't know about what we're collecting. The goal, however, is that we develop a data system that automates processes, elevates understanding, and helps us hit the bullseye with our decision-making.

As with each pillar of the *C.O.D.E.*, the key word is alignment. Your data processes must align with (be driven by) your KPI's. After all, if your data isn't influencing decisions that impact your KPI's, you're likely wasting your time.

A simple 3-step process for thinking about your data structure is:

1. What's the **question** I'm trying to answer?
2. What's the **process/plan** for getting to an informed answer?
3. What's the **action** once I have clear direction?
4. How does this **action** fuel further **questions**?

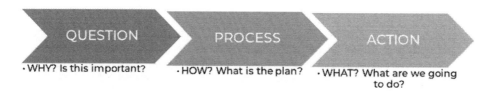

An example could be:

1. **Question**: How do I minimize/manage risk of non-contact injury?
2. **Process**: Collect data on the top risk factors/predictors of non-contact injury, and stratify them according to evidence-based norms to create a risk profile
3. **Action**: Develop individualized prescriptions for 'high risk' athletes to address need

Figure 7 is a *Feedback Loop* created by my colleague, Jesse Green, that can be used to organize data processes, and ultimately guide decision-making.

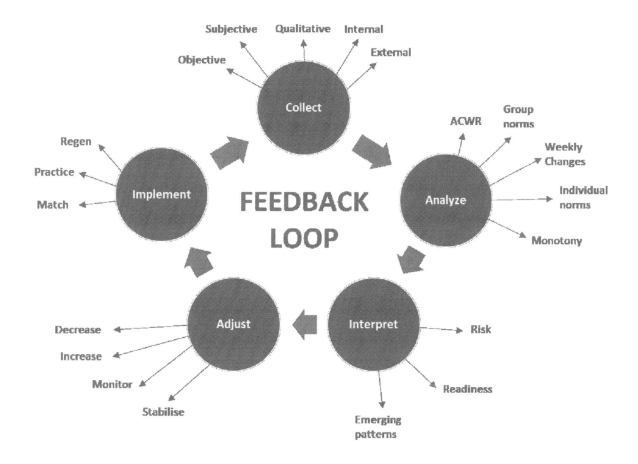

Figure 7. Feedback Loop

Execution (E)

Last, but not least, the fourth pillar of the **Performance C.O.D.E**. is EXECUTION. At the end of the day, we can accumulate vast knowledge, possess many shiny toys, and construct very impressive frameworks, and still not execute with impact. Why? Because execution is mostly about the 'soft' stuff- relationships, emotional intelligence, self and social awareness, and communication.

EXECUTION is obviously situation- and environment-specific and knowing your environment and your audience will always be essential for success. However, we are learning more each day about *HOW* to communicate more effectively- especially with millennials, *HOW* to build psychological safety (the cornerstone of all relationships), *HOW* to motivate (and *HOW* not to), and *HOW* to lead the new-age way. Just like the other pillars in the *C.O.D.E.*, *EXECUTION* strategies must be contemplated, organized, and operationalized for excellence.

There was a time (not long ago) when I thought *EXECUTION* was the art of the science; where the science came to life through the creative delivery of the coach. I now see *EXECUTION* as the perfect union of both art and science.

My *EXECUTION* strategies have always been organized around the same four words (written on the pillars in our facility at Louisville)- educate, motivate, inspire and empower. I believe coaches do all these four all the time, but great coaches think intensely about *HOW*.

Simply, *EXECUTION* is all about relationships, which take time. There are no shortcuts to establishing trust. However, as a reminder, the key to success in relationships (individual or team) is trust. Patrick Lencioni called an absence of trust the first dysfunction of a team (*The 5 Dysfunctions of a Team*), and after years of researching its top performing teams, *Google's Project Aristotle* concluded that the separating factor was psychological safety (or trust).

My recent views on *EXECUTION* around motivation, inspiration and empowerment have been shaped by Daniel Pink's book, *Drive*. In it, he discusses motivational science, and identifies autonomy, mastery, and purpose as the three 'drivers' of engagement. No more carrots and sticks! What is clear: motivating with a focus on shared purpose and shared consciousness is the new black. Helping people (athletes, teams, colleagues) realize they are part of something bigger than themselves (and reminding them constantly) is priority 1-10. Next, the key is to create an environment (workout spaces for athletes, work environments for staff members) where the shared purpose is lived, autonomy is promoted, and connection is fostered.

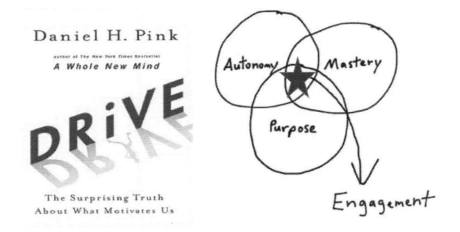

In *Culture Code*, Daniel Coyle also discusses the importance of leading with purpose and the parallel importance of environment. He references *Google* and *Zappos* as great examples of companies that prioritize nurturing a safe environment to drive connection, 'collision' and ultimately community, as well as risk taking and learning from failure. In performance terms, this means the need to think about where and how your athletes come in the door, and how you encourage and/or support failure. If you're a director, think about how you shape your meetings and where you put the coffee machine!

On the topic of mastery, we know that people leave leaders and cultures, not jobs. As a leader, if you care about your people and retention, you must create an environment (and a budget) that supports the path to mastery. I've heard some leaders say, '*What if we invest in our people and they leave?*' I like to remind them of Richard Branson's (Virgin Airlines) line, '*What if we don't and they stay!*'

Elevating *EXECUTION* also relies on communication, of course. However, where words are concerned, we now know that saying less, but rather asking and listening more is key. As the human attention span continues to shrink (now less than 8 seconds- less than a goldfish- according to Microsoft Corp.) we must be highly selective with when and

HOW we speak. We must also use "*sticky*" language and storytelling to be heard and remembered (see *Made to Stick* by Chip & Dan Heath)

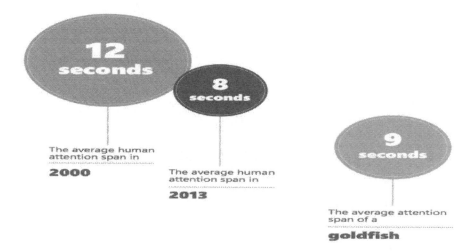

Figure 8. Average Human Attention Span (2015)

On the communication front, we also know that neural connections aren't made when people are being told what to do but are made during engaged reflection. This should lead us to prioritizing AAR's (After Action Reviews) and other forms of debriefing to deliver and request feedback, and ultimately guide change. On that front, *The Coaching Habit: Say Less, Ask More & Change the Way You Lead Forever* (by Michael Bungay Stanier) shares seven coaching questions for a variety of situations (from *The Kickstart Question* to *The Lazy Question*) to help us build stronger connections with our athletes (and co-workers) and ultimately get better results.

Finally, our views on *EXECUTION* are often shaped by our views on leadership, so as we rethink our strategies on one, we must rethink our strategies on the other. Shifting toward a transformational leadership (versus transactional) approach is essential if we are committed to adopting the **Performance C.O.D.E.**, as the qualities of one mirror the other.

Summary

In closing, the **Performance C.O.D.E.** is not meant to revolutionize or even disrupt the important work you do. Rather, it is a means for simplifying, aligning and hopefully enhancing your operation. Unlike your *WHY*, which should always stay the same, your

HOW should always be evolving (as you learn and grow). This framework provides you with a template for building and refining, personalizing and perfecting your *HOW*, now and into the future. That should be your competitive advantage.

Who is Teena Murray?

Teena Murray is in her first year as Senior Director of Athlete Health & Performance with the NBA's Sacramento Kings. In this new role she is charged with building a high-performance ecosystem to integrate a growing portfolio of elite performance services for Kings' players.

Prior to joining the Kings, Teena spent 14 years building a premiere program in collegiate athletics at the University of Louisville, that included an international mentorship program and an extensive performance analytics division. At Louisville, Teena was also an adjunct lecturer in the College of Health and Sport Science; and held an associate appointment in the Department of Bioengineering.

Teena brings over 22 years of experience as an educator, researcher, mentor and practitioner in the sports performance industry. Prior to Louisville, she held positions at the University of Connecticut and Cornell University. Outside the collegiate ranks, Teena has worked with several pro hockey (NHL) teams, the International Ice Hockey Federation, and from 2006-2010 was the Director of Performance for the U.S. Women's National and Olympic Hockey Teams.

Teena holds a Master's degree in Exercise Physiology & Sports Nutrition from the University of North Carolina at Greensboro, and undergraduate degrees in Education and Kinesiology from Queen's University (Canada) and Laurier University (Canada). She holds a long list of industry certifications, and is currently enrolled in an Executive Leadership Program at Northwestern University.

Teena believes in contributing to the field as a researcher and has 10 peer-reviewed publications. Her research centers on risk and performance profiling of elite athletes.

She is currently co-authoring a chapter on off-season training with Derek Hanson for the second edition of High-Performance Sport.

Teena is a native of Shawville, Quebec (Canada). Her and her partner Kellie have two daughters, MacKay (12) and Hadley (7).

2

Differences Between Tactical and Collegiate Strength and Conditioning

Andrew White MS, CSCS

KBRWyle Human Performance Specialist

MARSOC

In collegiate strength and conditioning you are physically preparing your athletes for the game. In tactical strength and conditioning you are physically preparing your athletes for "war". I will do my best to describe the differences between these two fields of strength and conditioning based on my personal experience training athletes in both realms. My hope with this chapter is to provide meaningful information to a prospective collegiate strength coach looking to make the move to tactical strength and conditioning. I also want tactical strength coaches to read this chapter and see how my opinions and approach differ from their situations, with the goal of creating an open dialogue amongst tactical strength and conditioning coaches.

In my experience there are three major differences between tactical and collegiate strength and conditioning; the athletes, the training, and the realities (salaries, working hours, etc.). I will be using the words "tactical" and "collegiate" to distinguish between the two types of strength and conditioning throughout the rest of the chapter. Again, everything I am going to be discussing in this chapter is my perspective only. When looking into different locations of tactical you may find few or many differences, just as in collegiate locations.

The Athlete

When describing the difference between a tactical athlete (focusing on military and special operations personnel, not fire fighters or law enforcement) and a collegiate athlete there a few things that I immediately noticed at my location. First, there are very few female athletes. Next, most of the athletes are Caucasian. Lastly, the tactical athlete will have some sort of shoulder, low back, or hip pain/immobility. These three things should not necessarily sway you in one way or the other from looking at a tactical job, but they are interesting to note if you happen to start looking into a tactical setting as a future employment opportunity. Along with the demographics of a tactical athlete you will find that they wear combat boots everywhere that is not called the "fitness center" and even then you might get a few people that wear their "boots'n'utes" in the weight room.

From a pure athleticism standpoint, tactical athletes are in no way similar to collegiate athletes. This should come as no surprise, considering that those I train are in the military and the ones you train are on the playing field. You will find some collegiate athletes willing to join the different military branches in later years through ROTC or the military academies, but they are few and far between. What tactical athletes lack in athleticism they more than make up for in respect and motivation. I have never had a tactical athlete make an excuse, whine, or simply quit in a workout. Amaingly, the psyche of a tactical athlete can be their downfall because they are always in a "do more" state and can lack awareness when it comes to something as simple as a rest period. Very often I have had to program rest periods into the training session just to make sure that they understand their importance. Even though this trait of "never backing down" may be a strength coach's best friend, it speaks to a bigger concern that is ever present in a tactical setting: mental health. The behavioral and psychological consequences of being in and around war are prevalent and frightening when you look deeper at its effects on the tactical athletes with whom you could potentially work on a regular basis. Tactical strength coaches are the "first line of defense" when it comes to the mental health of military personnel, so there is a great opportunity to have an impact on those you train in tactical settings. The daily conversations that we have go beyond the sets and reps have the greatest effect. Showing you care goes a long way in the collegiate setting, but I would argue that it goes even farther in a tactical setting.

This consideration leads me to my next point and perhaps most important, which is the amount of time that should be spent teaching the individual athlete. In a collegiate setting you may get a handful of athletes truly interested in your program and who want to know the "why's" for your workouts. However, for the most part, they are forced to be there by their sport coach and so there is already a certain level of blind trust. In tactical venues, most if not all those you train are not required to come see you, and not being forced to train with you. Most of the units at my location do not mandate physical training (PT) with strength coaches so it is entirely up to the individual to schedule PT during the week, whenever that may be. All of the tactical athletes I train will eventually be out of my weight room for a long period of time (deployment) or completely (retiring from the military). So, self-sufficiency is a premium in a tactical setting. Being able to set up your athletes for success outside of the weight room from a training process perspective is so vital in the tactical setting. I would argue that being able to eloquently and clearly explain how to set up a simple training cycle with appropriate exercises will ensure those athletes have the requisite technique and awareness to lift safely and correctly for a lifetime. I commonly come into contact with tactical athletes who are so beaten up and dysfunctional simply from utilizing poor form for all of the major lifts we utilize as strength coaches. Education is the greatest asset a tactical strength coach has, so it would be wise for strength coaches attempting to acquire a tactical job to have a thorough understanding and ability to explain standard strength training principles and the effectiveness of proper program design. This should not cause you hesitation from pursuing a tactical job, and, in all honesty, I feel explaining why I do what I do in my programming has made me a better strength coach and it will be a practice I would encourage any strength coach to adopt when working with their own athletes either in the collegiate or tactical field.

The age of the athletes I train range from 18 years old to 65 years old. This age range is so diverse because I work with combat support staff as well as entry level soldiers new to the SOF (Special Operation Forces) community, which I will describe a little later in the training section of this chapter. In a collegiate setting you are typically looking at an average age of 19-22 years for athletes in their prime, whereas when I look at the elite soldiers in tactical their prime age is between 24-30 years. With this age difference you there is a higher level of maturity and sense of ownership from a tactical athlete, which could be due in part to the tactical athlete having a fully developed frontal cortexes in their "prime." Many of the tactical athletes with whom I work are married and have children. Since tactical athletes are typically a little older than collegiate athletes I have noticed that their ability to learn new skills takes longer than when I was dealing with collegiate athletes. Specifically, I found this difference to be the result of three factors: a) most of the military athletes lack any athletic background, b) there is a limited amount of time with tactical athletes for proper skill development and, c) the difference in the lack of proper formal weight training leading up to their prime age, making the old habits a challenge to overcome. Now that I've given you a thorough explanation for the kind of "athlete" commonly encountered within a tactical setting, I want to go deeper into the actual training, or program design, differences between the two settings.

The Training

I began this op-ed with what I believe is the biggest and most obvious difference between collegiate and tactical, that being the end goal of the training. In the tactical setting there is no question the athletes are being prepared for "war". I put war in quotation marks because that might mean something different from person to person in a tactical weight room. As I mentioned in the previous section, I deal primarily with combat support staff in my role as a tactical strength coach. Most if not all of the personnel I train have previously seen or will never see a "typical" battlefield scenario. More often than not I train those people who work in the office setting or in warehouses whose job is to make sure the current soldiers on deployment have all of the resources needed to actually "pull the trigger". There are also some opportunities for me to train the "bad asses of the world" (think Seals, Rangers, Operators, etc.) or those coming up in the ranks of special operations (think selects and candidates going through the pipeline to get into the SOF units). Most tactical jobs involve a greater degree of one or the other. In my environment, there are strength coaches who deal primarily with elite fighters and there are those such as in my job who deal with a wide array of tactical athletes. When designing a program for top-level individuals or combat support staff a common-sense approach to the training must be taken. Typically, I try to stay on a linear progression model that relies heavily on progressive overload principles. This program design allows the user to come back to the program at any point and "start over" with new maxes based on how they feel on that particular day. As can be imagined the programs I write in my tactical location are different than my approach with collegiate athletes in the past where I had distinct training phases that correlated to a sport season.

Every strength coach has foundational principles that they use to produce a program for the athletes they train. Tactical is no different but the pieces of the proverbial puzzle when looking at a periodization model, if you will, are different from the collegiate setting. When I was first interviewed for my current job I was asked a question that I honestly did not know how to answer. The question was, "How would you train a tri-athlete?" Initially, that seemed an easy enough question to answer. However, it was followed by "now assume the tri-athlete would have over 60 lbs. on them." Immediately I started racing through the rolodex of my mind to all the previous athletes with whom

I worked and the different training methods I used, but from my time in tactical the answer to that question is now abundantly clear: training must cover everything, which sounds really cliché, but it is the absolute truth. So, tactical can give a strength coach the feeling that no aspect is being trained exceptionally well because of the extreme concern about the athletes being prepared for anything. However, if I was to choose one adaptation a tactical athlete requires more than anything, I would propose the need for absolute strength. Strength is always king and allows anyone to handle whatever they encounter; so, I put a premium on that training adaptation. A co-worker of mine always states a belief that I believe to be the most accurate depiction (good, bad, or indifferent) of what the training philosophy is in tactical: "You are training these guys in a controlled environment (weight room) to be ready in an uncontrolled one (battlefield), so don't worry about being too specific."

Those words have always guided my outlook in my programming approach and it speaks to the difference in specificity between tactical and collegiate training. Tactical training is general almost throughout the entire training process, whereas in a collegiate setting the starting pout would obviously be general while working to more specific training when the athletes are closer to their sport season. There is no realistic way for me to provide specific training for someone who diffuses bombs on a regular basis or who has to train foreign military personnel about how to be real soldiers. At times having a limited basis for how to specifically train these tactical athletes to complete their jobs can be frustrating as a strength coach. In desiring to provide the best program possible, it is difficult to accomplish when the nature of tactical training is general at best. I have found that micro-dosing helps the tactical athletes with whom I come into contact on a daily basis. Being able to hit a lot of training adaptations at once is not really optimal but helps to create the adaptations we want over time. I will have guys come in that can only train for 15 minutes and others that may be able to train for an hour and a half. So, when looking at the key performance indicators for that individual or group, I start with the most important ones (typically overall strength) and hit the others when we have more time. Also, considering the approach of being general at best, almost all of the tactical athletes I have encountered need an extensive amount of time simply working on the basics. Merely going through the bench (flat and incline), deadlift (trap bar and barbell), and squat (front and back) progressions will attain substantial results in a tactical setting.

With the training process in tactical being general there are some situations in this area that will allow work towards a more specific goal. Most of these goals will come in the form of physical goals, such as increasing pull ups or wanting to fit into the uniform a little better for their promotion pictures (a serious observation). So, I want to state as clearly as possible that sometimes there exists the impression of being a personal trainer! This might be considered an alarming thought because strength coaches should never be grouped with personal trainers, right? So, I want to offer the advice I never received before I started training in the tactical setting. This aspect of tactical has been particularly challenging for me to handle at times and I wish I would have known that these situations would arise up. In my location I have to put on a personal training "hat" much more than I would like, and that is why I alluded to self-sufficiency being so important in tactical. Even though personal training may occur for a little bit, the goal is to effectively tool that individual to make workout plans for themselves instead of succumbing to doing what they used to do, which, more often than not, led them to be injured and over-trained.

Although being a personal trainer at times will occur, there will of course be opportunities to be a strength coach and "get after it" in the weight room. Most of the strength coaches who work with elite level tactical athletes enjoy these sessions regularly. So, when are applying for a tactical job try to find out which kind of units (combat support staff, elite Special Forces, office workers, civilian contractors) could eventually be your targeted training as that could potentially indicate how much "personal training" will be required to implement.

Exercise	Notes	Week 1 Sets	Week 1 Reps	Week 1 Load	Week 2 Sets	Week 2 Reps	Week 2 Load	Week 3 Sets	Week 3 Reps	Week 3 Load	Week 4 Sets	Week 4 Reps	Week 4 Load
Performance Preparation	Superset Exercises												
HK Band Row		3	8-12		3	8-12	0	3	8-12		3	8-12	0
TRX "Y"		3	10		3	10	0	3	10		3	10	0
Bench Press	Light to Heavy	3	10,8,6		3	10,8,6	0	3	10,8,6		3	10,8,6	0
Primary Training Block													
Bench Press (5 sec. negative)	Weeks 1 & 2:	4	3	75	4	3	80	4	3	75	4	3	80
Clapping Push Up	5 second Eccentric	4	3		4	3	0	4	3		4	3	0
Med Ball Throw	Weeks 3 & 4:	4	3		4	3	0	4	3		4	3	0
AFSM Dumbbell Push Up	5 second Isometric	4	3		4	3	0	4	3		4	3	0
				0			0			0			0
Secondary Training Block	Not a Superset												
TRX Inverted Row	Feet Elevated	3	8		2	10	0	2	9		2	8	0
Rest 1-2 Min. BTWN Each Set													0
Pull Ups		2	AMAP		2	AMAP	0	2	AMAP		2	AMAP	0
													0
0	Heavy	1	12	0	1	10	0	1	8	0			0
Auxiliary Training Block	Superset Exercises												
Barbell Bent Over Row		2-4	15		2-4	12	0	2-4	10		2-4	8	0
Dumbbell Shoulder Press		2-4	15		2-4	12	0	2-4	10		2-4	8	0
Front Delt Raise		2-4	15		2-4	12	0	2-4	10		2-4	8	0
Plank with Arm Lift		2-4	15s		2-4	20's	0	2-4	25's		2-4	30's	0
Post Workout Recovery	Mobility WOD												

Fig. 1: Example of an Upper Body Max Strength Block.

I wanted to include this snapshot of an Upper Body Max Strength Block (Figure 1) that I have used to train the high-level athletes I see from time to time. Typically, I would have liked to focus on one training goal (isometric training) during a 4 week to 2-month span but I have found 2 week blocks to be the most effective in tactical because of limited time, which speaks to the way my training programs move from one aspect to the next in the desire to cover my bases (micro-dosing), while at the same time keeping the program relatively general. When developing the workout above my main emphasis was upper body max strength; so, my goal when going through this workout is to complete the performance preparation block, either from the workout itself or from the general one (shown later in this chapter) used for that week. The performance preparation helps the individual prepare for the main movement in the workout by stressing the antagonist muscles to the main movement, as well as engaging the core. After the performance preparation block the next step would naturally be to move on to the primary training block. In the primary training block, the most important work for the day takes place. After the primary training block is complete, the individual would then have the choice to complete the rest of the prescribed training blocks or be done for the day. At this point I give the individual autonomy to choose movements that correspond with exercises I have programmed for the remaining training blocks. So, looking at the workout example, in the secondary training block I have programmed TRX Inverted Rows (a horizontal row) and Pull Ups (a vertical row). The individual can choose any horizontal or vertical row they would like, but they have to stick to the set and rep scheme I have programmed. When I let the individual athlete choose their own exercises it provides a great teaching moment. Letting them know there is more than one way to do things as long as they have a strategy behind the programming (intent) and to keep the workout fun and interesting is what I really want that individual to understand.

When lookin at the training example, some undertones of Cal Dietz's Tri-Phasic Training, as well as Joe Kenn's Tier System should be evident. These two training methods have been great tools that I use on a regular basis. I have found some tri-phasic components to be great tools in helping me coach the movement patterns at the beginning of a training phase. Throughout the slow and hold (eccentric and isometric portions) movements I am able to highlight the importance of tension and proper alignment throughout the entirety of a lift. It is during this slow movement athletes forget the benefits of tension and stability during the lift, and tri-phasic has helped bring that training effect to life.

Along with tri-phasic implementation, simple characteristics of the Tier System have allowed me to explain the training process. In tactical, a strength coach does not always have the luxury to prescribe specific stress types for each individual workout (Upper body, Lower body, etc.). Although the above training session isn't a total body session, I like to follow the Tier System's approach to total body training. Putting a priority on certain movements and blocks has taught the tactical athletes with whom I work to prioritize their training when time is limited, and fully understand the intent of the entire workout when they have more time.

Also, the staff at my location and I have recently started to see the value of a good warm-up and its effects on the rest of the training process. So, we began structuring our "warm-up process" based upon the work of Dr. Rusin and his 6 Phase Dynamic Warm Up. Of course, there are some elements that we retained and others that we modified to fit our location and the athletes we train. The order of the different parts within his warmup protocol were maintained.

General Dynamic Warm Up	**Performance Preparation**
Jog Down and Back (20 yards) x 4 Forward Skip/Backward Skip (20 yards) x 2 Side Shuffle (20 yards) x 2 Over Hurdles x 6 each way Hamstring w/T-Spine Rotation x 10 yards Ankle Plantar & Dorsiflexion 5 x 3 sec. each way Iron Cross & Scorpion x 5 each way	*Upper Body* - Shoulder Taps 2 x 6 – 8 each - Single Arm TRX Row 2 x 8 – 12 - Banded Mountain Climbers 2 x 8-12 each - Specific Warm Up Sets *Squat Patterns* - Slide Board Glute Ham Raise 2 x 8-12 each - Miniband Clamshell 2 x 8-12 each - Split Squat Single Kettlebell Hold 2 x 10 sec. each side - Specific Warm Up Sets *Hinge Patterns* - Single Leg Pistol Squat 2 x 8-12 each - Band Pull Through 2 x 8-12 - Glute Ham Swimmers 2 x 10 each side - Specific Warm Up Sets
Post Workout Cool Down ***Ask Strength Coach for*** **Recommendations**	

Figure 2. Dynamic Warm Up and Performance Preparation Example

When looking at the left side of the diagram you will see our general dynamic warm up. This setup is focused on general movement (first three exercises) and then goes into range of motion work (next four movements). The four range of motion exercises are based upon recommendations from the physical therapists who work with us. The areas in which tactical athletes experience the most problems (hips, thoracic spine, and ankles) are the main sources of the range of motion work we complete. Also, on the left side of the diagram is the section labeled "post workout cool down." We treat this on an individual basis with a strength coach's recommendation. Typically, when addressing cool down procedures, we want to get the individual into a parasympathetic state as quickly as possible to start the process of adaptation. So, we employ modalities that help achieve that goal and educate the user to be aware of what works for them. A very common tool we use in the cool down period is simple breathing mechanics and establishing the good belly breath technique while manipulating the breathing tempo.

When looking at the right side of the diagram you will see our "performance preparation." I alluded to this performance preparation period earlier when discussing the training example. The performance preparation is meant to target specific areas of the body to prepare for the main movement for the day, which is why the last exercise in each section is labeled "specific warm up sets". The specific warm up sets will be the same as the main movement for the day, such as barbell bench press, trap bar deadlift, or back squat. We have broken down our performance preparation into three main categories of movement, again with the help of Dr. Rusin, and specifically, his foundational movement progressions. We primarily look at the Upper Body, Squat, and Hinge movements. It is through this warmup that our staff feels our athletes will be ready to complete any work they are prescribed in the weight room.

The structured training sessions seen in the collegiate setting (weekly training blocks- undulating periodization, post season, pre-season, etc.) are not common in tactical. The training of athletes in tactical is entirely up to each strength coach or "SME" (subject matter expert). This is a great option but also very complicated because it can be difficult to understand what can be positively affected in the amount of time available with an individual or group. Also, a lot of military personnel have a requirement called TAD (Temporary Assigned Duty) that needs to be completed throughout the year, thus removing them from the weight room for 2-4 weeks at various times. On a group level, training sessions can be scheduled for upwards of 6 months out of the year (this is the longest I have had a group) but of those available training days the whole group will only be available for about 60-75% of the training phase. So, a tactical training program needs to be highly adaptable or provide different options that the individual could ultimately choose on any particular day within a pre-determined training phase. For example, if the primary interest is to develop max strength but an individual or group can only be seen three times a week for three months, it might be best to micro dose other methods on top of the main focus in hopes of creating a small change numerous of fronts to make the athletes more resilient. The group training aspects in tactical provides a great opportunity to develop and educate a lot of tactical athletes at once. It is from this platform that tactical strength coaches may have their greatest impact.

All of the preceding paragraphs on training has been focused on while the tactical athlete is here at home with available weight rooms and strength coaches (typically). When tactical athletes are home they are tasked with a host of other duties and responsibilities that makes their time in the weight room sparse and at times non-existent. However, if you had to pinpoint when a tactical athlete is in their "off-season" it is actually when they are deployed. When tactical athletes are on deployment they typically have much more time to devote to an actual training plan, depending on the job they have of course. So, there are challenges with this considering it from a strength coach perspective. First, the athletes lacking contact with their strength coach, it is difficult to assume that the athletes will know exactly the desired goals from workout to workout. This is very similar to prescribing a fall sports team a workout during the end of spring into summer and trusting they look at the program once or twice. This speaks to the self-sufficiency piece I have noted earlier and how important it is. Next, there is limited communication when tactical athletes are abroad, for obvious reasons. Usually if they are reaching out to individuals back at home it is family and friends, not their strength coach. Third, they have limited resources overseas to complete the training programs created for them. Some will be stationed on foreign military bases which will have most if not all of the necessary equipment. Others will be in remote areas and will only be able to use "fly-away kits" where the equipment is limited to the weight they can pack onto the plane. Finally, load management is an issue overseas because of the time the athletes will have, so it is extremely important for a tactical strength coach to program specifically the times to "crush yourself" and get two perhaps three workouts in a day and when to cut back and complete one workout in a day or take a rest day. As always, intent should drive the programming and when tactical athletes are overseas that emphasis needs to be driven home clearly and concisely.

Lastly, from a training perspective, there are some considerations for which tactical strength coaches need to account that are not necessarily tied directly to their training programs, but speaks more to the dogma of a military setting. Those components are standardized bodyweight measurements and physical fitness tests. The athletes with whom I work have two physical testing requirements they need to complete every year: Physical Fitness Test and the Combat Fitness Test. These assessments, which are not evaluated by strength coaches but by military personnel, strongly occupy the minds of those we train because these two arbitrary assessments can ultimately determine promotional opportunities. Along with the fitness tests there are physical bodyweight to height standards that need to be met. For example, a male who measures 5'9" in height cannot exceed 186 lbs. and can be no less than 128 lbs. These bodyweight to height standards can become problematic when an individual simply doesn't conform to the typical military body type.

At its most basic level the consistency of any strength training program is the most to be imagined as a strength coach. In the tactical setting getting these athletes to keep using your program and not some CrossFit or bodybuilding program is doing themselves and the "Command" (military unit) a great service. Again, when tactical athletes use programs on their own, they typically utilize faulty movement patterns and over-train certain areas, primarily the hips, shoulders, and low backs. In my opinion this point cannot be stressed enough. From an athlete-training perspective, education of the training process and correct movement patterns to mitigate injury from the start are the most important aspects of tactical strength and conditioning. Now that I have described the difference between the athlete and the training, I want to shift gears and examine the actualities of the job is different.

The Realities

In considering the differences between one job and another, salary is a primary factor. In analyzing the National Strength and Condition Association's Coaches Survey published in October 2018, the average salary for those in tactical positions is listed as slightly less than $70,000 ($69,437 to be exact). That number alone might drive some coaches to consider tactical jobs. This number usually means everyone on that particular tactical strength staff will make this salary because they are civilian contractors. A civilian contractor is paid through a contracting company that wins a bid to be the provider of services to the government/military agent. Regardless of the experience a person does or does not possess, every strength coach on a tactical staff will more than likely have an identical salary. There are some tactical positions that are higher on the pay scale for that particular military branch which would allow more money to be earned. Sometimes these jobs are GS, meaning General Schedule or on the government payroll and these jobs are established in the government's budget. With that being the case these positions become very hard to eliminate, so if job security is a premium for a coaching, seeing a GS tactical positions would be recommended. There is obvious insecurity when it comes to collegiate jobs because of the fickle nature of athletics, the insecurity of a tactical job is not knowing whether the government will continue to allocate funds from the federal budget to allow your contracting company to keep providing jobs for those people filling positions. This situation occurred at my location before I started working here, and the strength staff was essentially cut by 30-40% without any substantial warning.

Along with salary differences, the procurement of equipment or acquiring continuing education for your weight room/staff is different between settings. In college, purchases need to be precisely determined because the athletic department budget is contained by the needs of the varying sports under that umbrella. At most collegiate locations the relationship between the head strength coach and the athletic director would be a crucial factor. Otherwise utilizing equipment that is a decade old is an extreme likelihood. In tactical there always seems to be more than enough money to go around, but the obstacles to be navigated for big ticket items can become an annoyance. Also, it can be hard to convince Congress that a weight room is valuable which can be problematic at times for the military units wanting to have strength coaches. From a continuing education standpoint, we are able to choose whomever we want, but the actual speaker has to go through the government protocols to be compensated, which can cause the process to seemingly crawl. Also, my contracting company allocates a specific amount of money for their employees to go to conferences, this is similar to some collegiate S&C departments.

The next reality I would like to describe is the actual workday. The "grind" of a collegiate strength and conditioning coach is well-documented. Working extensive hours such as from 6am to 8pm or a similar time-intensive schedule. My goal is not to propose whether this is good or bad, but I can attest that tactical is less extensive from a structured schedule standpoint. My schedule is 9am to 5pm, which that is a benefit of being a civilian contractor. The other strength coaches at my location work from 5am to 1pm. Along with the actual working hour difference are the non-traditional workdays that collegiate coaches are asked to complete, those being weekends and holidays. Football and basketball strength coaches typically miss out of Thanksgivings and Christmases with their immediate/extended families and must attend team functions instead. With the connection to a specific team, this is understandable.

In tactical weekends and all federal holidays are not worked, as well as paid time off (usually two full weeks at most locations). Considering those few, some S and C job seekers might have heightened interest. However, if you greatly enjoy the idea of game day, you will miss that exhilaration when working with tactical athletes. There are no games to anticipate, chances to win a ring, team dinners, award banquets, or the enjoyment of taking a team from off-season workouts through post-season tournaments. On the other hand, tactical provides an appropriate way to obtain a work/life balance, on that may be worth exploring.

I

Figure 3. The weight room at my location

In addition to the salary and working hour differences, I would like to shift to the structure of how the facility is operated and run. When considering the actual coaching component, being a disciplinarian in a tactical setting is never a concern. For certain, intensity will need to be displayed to "fire up" the athletes, but the need to discipline a tactical athlete will never occur. Too often I remember sport coaches relying on strength coaches to be the "bad guy" or the one who held the athletes accountable. In the tactical world the rare adult who requires discipline will receive it from a supervisor other than the S and C coach. This factor speaks to the structure of the groups you would train in tactical. Instead of working together with a sport coach, a unit leader who determines the daily schedule for the individuals going through that particular course or training will be the primary contact person in tactical. As such the group leader would sit down with the strength coach and determine when would be the best time for their group to get PT completed. In elite units there are team leaders who facilitate this for their groups, but they always coordinate with the strength coach. At my location everyone wants to schedule groups between 0500 and 0800 (got to love military time) or from 1500 to 1700. These times correspond to the individual's actual work schedule which are consistently from 0800 to 1500, with chow being from 1100 to 1300.

I believe this final factor is especially crucial. Tactical is driven by data, and more accurately utilization, while collegiate is driven by wins and losses. In the tactical setting the validity of these S and C positions are based upon supervisors and supervisors generating statistics to prove the worthiness of your position. The government, understandably, wants to ensure the taxpayer's money is being utilized to produce the desired results. The tactical data of greatest interest is the utilization of the program and injury rates. The assumption is that those who use our programs will ultimately have lower injuries and thus those tactical athletes can continue to be an asset for that military branch. As such, the reliance on data at my location is of utmost importance and can be quite overwhelming at times. At other locations I know they have not been tasked with this degree, but the future of tactical can be verified with data. There certainly exists a correlation between the funding allocated and the desire to maintain the extended readiness of the tactical athletes to perform the required duties and expectations.

Conclusion

Throughout this chapter, I have provided examples regarding the differences between a tactical strength and conditioning job and a collegiate strength and conditioning position. Tactical athletes come in many shapes, sizes, and ages. It is the job of the tactical strength coach to take these things and provide a program that a) works for the command/mission for whom they work and b) keeps the user coming back each day. There must be an awareness of the dogmatic military structure and the level at which the strength and conditioning component fit within that hierarchy.

Upon addressing the user portion of this job, the actual training is typically determined by the individual coach. I have proposed what has and continues to work for me at my particular location. In whatever training methods others may choose to employ clear and concise principles to educate that individual or group, with self-sufficiency being the ultimate goal, need to be determined

Is a tactical job different from a collegiate job? As explained in detail the positions are indeed different in many vital aspects. From salaries to working hours to numerous other factors, these two fields couldn't be more dissimilar. With that being said both positions will always entail being a strength coach. Enthusiastic and vigorous coaching are key for all athletes: love and coach them as "family".

My desire has been to pull back the curtain on the mysterious tactical strength and conditioning field. Open positions can be readily seen while scrolling through Indeed.com or from openings shared through word of mouth amongst colleagues. Of course, each location is different, and my experience has been limited to my current assignment. However, my goal has been to focus on a few considerations I have determined through my work in this field.

One final thought is the severity and inherent danger that comes with the job of the tactical athletes themselves. The stark reality of tactical can at times be a little overwhelming when those you train one day do not return. This grim circumstance is always a sobering aspect. In summation, tactical strength and conditioning, as with collegiate strength and conditioning, can be rewarding environments in which to work, and thus far, I am excited about the path I have taken in which I progress, having experienced the distinct and self-determined advantages and disadvantages of both venues.

Who is Andrew White?

Andrew White is a Tactical Performance Specialist for KBRWyle, working at Camp Lejuene in North Carolina. He has been in this role for the past 3 years and works primarily with the MARSOC branch of the Special Operation Force community.

Prior to this current post, Andrew was an Assistant Strength Coach at the University of Richmond where he oversaw the training of the women's tennis, field hockey, and women's soccer programs. Also, during his time in Richmond, Andrew assisted with high school swim athletes for the swim club NOVA of Virginia Aquatics in their dry-land development.

A graduate of the Ohio State University (bachelors) and the University of Cincinnati (masters), Andrew draws much of his influence on program design and athletic development from the likes of DeMayo, Jennings, the Verkhoshansky's, Yessis, Everett, Rippetoe, and Bondarchuk, among others.

3

The Performance Director's Secret Soft Syllabus

The Foundation of all Good Performance-Communication

Fergus Connolly

Performance Expert

The greatest mistake we make in performance today is not realizing that the effectiveness of our hard skills (sport science, strength and conditioning, speed technique etc.) is completely and utterly reliant on the quality of our soft skills.

Over the course of 15 years working with professionals across elite sport, business and military, I learned through much failure that to be successful I had to develop a certain set of secret and vague 'soft' skills in order to be truly effective and to lead and manage people in high performance. This secret skillset was a completely different set of abilities or exam subjects to the performance skillsets I had developed as a professional. As one of the first performance directors, I realized there was a whole new set of leadership skills I was never taught through formal education.

Now as I mentor and advise the next generation of professionals in sport, military, and the corporate world, it's apparent these skillsets are the ones that either ensure you will succeed or struggle and perhaps fail in your role as the head of a department, high performance manager, athletic director, performance director, or whatever leadership role to which you aspire.

These experiences led me to write a syllabus and course for Performance Directors and in this chapter, I will focus on only one - Communication

Communication – an Introduction

All good performance directors have good basic communication skills. It's a given. Some are excellent at addressing crowds, others have great personalities and build great relationships, and a few have both, but I've not seen one performance director succeed for any period of time without the ability to communicate well in some form.

Most continue to develop these skills as their careers progress. It's virtually impossible to be a good leader, or even practitioner, with poor communication ability, whether that's to players, staff, or front office.

Communication as an overall skill is not complex, but the more you understand and consider communication the greater the adaptability, effectiveness and sustainability of your messages. We interact casually with staff on a daily basis, we present ourselves nonverbally through body language, we send emails, use handouts, and text possibly hundreds of times a day in total. All of these are instances of communication – it's far more powerful than you might first imagine.

Why we communicate

It's important just to touch briefly on the purpose of our communication for a moment. As a performance director our goal is to lead, deliver messages, provide information, and help educate players, staff, and front office.

Staff

With our staff the key function is to listen to and understand the challenges they face. We need to concisely explain the goals and objectives for each one of them and the department as a whole. They generally are the easiest with whom to communicate even though they may have different skills but still speak our language since they underwent similar education stages.

Senior Management

With the front office the clear needs are to unmistakably understand their requirements of you and your role, and the deliverables they want presented. In many cases their backgrounds may be different than ours. They come from a varied background of education, business, and even playing careers.

Players

Players on the other hand require support, direction, and understanding of actions that will support their performance goals and allow them to perform optimally on and off the field or court. In this case we often need to gain trust and build habits that allow them to continue to improve.

Backroom Bandwidth

Each group has different back grounds, objectives, and goals. I refer to this as 'backroom bandwidth'. There is a different need for each. However, with careful consideration it's very possible to create a communication approach which can address all groups in a very cohesive way. Nonetheless it requires a careful understanding.

Learning from Others

Bill Clinton

Bill Clinton had a special ability to get his point across to both large groups and individuals. He used two distinct styles, but both based on the same philosophy. In groups he made a special point to demonstrate to the audience he understood their concerns and fears by verbalizing them. With individuals he connected on a personal level by listening, giving them full attention and taking time to ensure they felt heard. These approaches allowed him to establish an emotional connection with his audiences. One unique aspect of Clinton's approach you should learn from was his communication never seemed trite or gimmicky because of his attention to and connection with his audience. We can use these approaches, especially his ability to gain trust and connect by listening and demonstrating our genuine interest in the audience.

Winston Churchill

Winston Churchill has been long regarded as a great communicator. He is especially well-known for his one-liners or catch phrases. He used short impactful statements such as 'Attitude is a little thing that makes a big difference', and 'Never, Never, Never.' This often overlooks the importance of his ability to create an image for the audience. Unlike Clinton he had little visual opportunities to influence his audience and relied on his voice across the radio to connect. As a performance director we can learn from Churchill's ability to portray authority in a strong voice and establish our own presence.

Donald Trump

Donald Trump is a very effective communicator for two particular reasons. He exploits emotional concerns and targets fears to elicit a response from his audience. He also uses mediums like twitter to deliver short phrases that are clear in message and attention grabbing. While I don't recommend this approach, we can learn from it. We can target emotional fears in athletes (injury fears, aging concerns) and use short clear unambiguous phrases to connect with them. We should also learn from the negative effect of Trump's approach by avoiding divisive or confusing messages.

Intrapersonal Communication

Before we start on what is regarded generally by everyone as 'communication,' I want to mention one often overlooked aspect. I've spoken about authenticity before and nowhere is it more important and evident than in communication. Authenticity and transparency in communication will ultimately determine your ability to build a sustainable program and maintain the trust of your audience.

Self-Talk

However, the most often ignored communication is what we say and hear from ourselves. Intrapersonal communication is communication with oneself. It can be audible, written, internal vocalization, and even reflective thinking. Your own voice is the most powerful voice you have, and the most convincing. Be alone with your own thoughts for a short period and you realize how powerful they are.

Authenticity in communication means having a clear and honest vision, objectives and aims. Verbalizing them to everyone, yourself included. A message that you neither believe in nor communicate will both undermine your own confidence and will easily become apparent to the people, players, staff and management with whom you interact.

The Communication Process

We rarely think of communication as a process, but it is actually an ongoing continuous process. Good performance directors are constantly aware of this and so continually recalibrate the impact of every message, verbal and non-verbal, and consider it a process. This is why I often refer to it as a 'campaign.'

As you become aware of how impactful communication is, it's equally important not to become self-conscious. Nonetheless, it's important to be self-aware of the full impact we have on others and the messages we send. In the performance context our human communication is generally an interpersonal process in which a message is relayed with a goal or intention to elicit or inspire a positive action.

While I don't suggest you plan all interactions in a very detailed manner, I want you to be aware that communication is a process and series of considerations.

Source

As the performance director you must ensure that, while not all messages need to come directly from you, you need to be aware of the messages of your staff and those that pertain to performance matters. You ultimately are responsible for the messages of the department and staff or at least will have to deal with misinformation. This is where the overall vision and ethos of the department is key.

You can't insist every message is approved or ran past you, but proper organization, meetings, and leadership will ensure you avoid this issue.

Medium

Usually when we consider communication, the first thing we think of is the medium. The medium is the immediate form which a message takes. We might use a presentation, posters, images, emails, or a quiet word one-on-one. We choose the medium largely on two factors: the audience receiving the message and the most suitable vehicle.

Vehicle

As the source of a message we must consider first of all if we are the best source to deliver a message. As the performance director, you don't have to be the voice constantly. If a staff member has a better relationship in relating to strength & conditioning, nutrition, or rehab, they may be the better vehicle for this message. The vehicle could be in-person, but it can be not only image-based, audio, or text, but a combination of these.

Audience

In other communication situations the audience is deemed responsible for interpreting and understanding the message, but in this industry the responsibility is on us to ensure the message is interpreted and understood. To achieve this, we must consider the audience perspective, mindset, medium, and vehicle most suited to them.

Audience Perspective

One of the biggest mistakes we make as performance directors is that we believe others want and interpret information in the same way as we do. However, we are very different from the audiences with whom we spend most of our time communicating. We've had a desire to understand things, we usually want detail, we need to be convinced in a way that supports a scientific understanding.

Players are generally used to a certain medium and vehicle of communication whereas coaches and other staff are familiar with a slightly different medium and vehicle. I disagree completely with the position that we must explain the 'how it works' so people will do something. Yes, for some populations this is needed, the playing audience does not require this. They want to know the 'what.'

The best place to be convinced of this is to look at what motivates the audience to whom you are speaking to and what motivates them to arrive with an inherent buy-in. Many athletes have had different educational backgrounds and experiences.

Multiple Audiences

In our profession we need to remember our messages rarely are delivered to one person, whether we plan it or not. The most effective communication strategy considers cohesiveness and uses themes to ensure a consistent message.

Context

A message delivered at the wrong time or incorrect location loses its power or even its point. Trying to deliver a message in a crowded room or busy street is largely a waste of time. Unless you consider the timing and location, your messages will fall to the same issues.

Context is critical not only to the delivery but also the interpretation. Communication is either reinforced or weakened by the environment in which it exists. The place, time, event, all impact the attitude of the audience regardless of the message itself. It's best to wait until the right moment and place to make a point you need remembered and taken on board.

Setting a New Context

While the actual context in which your audience finds itself is always important, you still have the power to manipulate and create the optimal context to present your message. This involves careful thought and creativity but delivered appropriately it can be very effective in terms of the overall winning strategy. For example, after a blow-out win where overconfidence is starting to creep in, a message of calm, caution, and humility can be reinforced if appropriately presented.

Strategies to do this can involve:

1. Giving the example of a team who lost focus, let standards in treatment, training, and practice slip and lost to a much lesser opponent the following week.
2. Relating a story of a team in a similar situation previously who then went on a losing streak.
3. Role-playing the possibility of everyone taking their eye off the ball and the consequences that might follow.

Strategies such as these can set a new context to deliver a message that might be in contrast to the mood or context of a situation in which an important message must be delivered without the benefit of time or when time constraints are an issue.

Feedback

Many performance directors have a 'fire and forget' attitude to communication. However, good communicators see this as the beginning of the end. They see it not just as an end but an ongoing process.

Always look for feedback but remember it doesn't have to be interpersonal. Asking for feedback can give an impression of a lack of confidence depending on who you ask, how you ask and also on the message being delivered. For a performance director authority is important.

Feedback can come from body language, posture, attention, questions, facial expression or reactions of the audience. I use a simple rule that any comments from a person mean that 'seven' others feel the same way or had a similar impression. Feedback doesn't have to be immediate. If you are running a 'campaign' it's best to wait until the campaign has been established before reacting to it.

Requesting Feedback

By all means, be aware of the influencers in the group. They can be those who are in positions of authority, but also be aware of those who are not directly in roles but are still influential, such as veterans or those who are not in senior positions but are vocal.

It's worth bearing in mind that all of your audience are not only different by role and position, but also by their interests, so not everything will appeal to each person. Expect and accept that some will respond positively, and some will not; do not be disheartened by some people who don't respond favorably.

Message

If everything has been considered the message should be short, concise, and delivered with clarity. This does not mean the interaction needs to be very short, but the actual message should be.

Set the scene

As you deliver the message bear in mind the mindset and perspective of the audience. Start from where they are: don't simply fire your message at them. Acknowledge their position or frame of mind and 'take them on a journey' from there.

For example, if you're addressing a group of players and you want them to come for treatment or check in the next morning after a late return flight, explain you know that they will be tired. It's important to acknowledge their concerns and placate to remove the excuse or put them at ease.

Explain the Benefit

Once you have identified their position, present the benefits to them - they get treatment done early and get more time off with the family. Note, I don't mention the benefit to you. I don't suggest you outline that, as a team or organization it's most important to find out the status of the players – speak to their concerns professionally. The reason is important, but it is not necessarily what they are concerned with.

Keep in mind that, these are all adults with free will and there has to 'be something in it for them', some benefit. However, more importantly, by getting them to decide and choose to do something there is a far greater chance of compliance and of establishing a routine or habit.

Delivery

Don't start your message without explaining the context or putting fears at ease first. Think of it as comparable to asking someone to take medicine. Before you explain 'what' you want someone to do, allay any fears, explain the benefits and present a solution.

Know very clearly what the key sentence is in your presentation, image or talk. Don't be afraid to repeat it. Mention it at the start, reinforce the benefit, and repeat again.

Consider it a 6-point loop:

1. Address the concerns of the audience
2. Explain what your message is
3. Explain the benefit to them
4. Explain what your message is
5. Address the concerns of the audience
6. Explain what your message is

You're presenting a solution, a benefit, to help them, and it must be framed as such.

Reinforcement

I never consider a message a singular event or action. A message should be always part of a larger program or campaign. There should always be a follow-up or a secondary supporting message or action to reinforce and remind. This may simply be in the form of a text, an image, or a comment in passing individually.

Noise

Noise is any factor that inhibits the delivery of your message, anything that gets in the way of the message being accurately received, interpreted, and acknowledged. These are distractions and noise that can affect the concentration, focus, and attention of the audience.

Noise can present an internal or external distraction. An athlete concerned about a contract extension may not be attentive or fully focused on the message you are trying to deliver because they are distracted by internal noise. Disturbances outside the room, external noise, may prevent the clear delivery of a message to an audience or individual.

Barriers to Effective Communication

There are six key things we should avoid as performance directors when communicating:

- Prejudging or not considering the audience
- Not having a good understanding of who you are targeting
- Not being aware of the audience's attention
- Using your terminology, not the audience's language
- Not delivering a message that the audience needs or giving unwanted advice
- Not concerned with or addressing the audience's needs or fears

Notice that all are concerned with the audience, not the messenger.

Keys to Effective Communication

There are key elements performance directors should remember when we communicate:

- Follow-up to reinforce with additional messages and/or actions
- Get feedback either verbally at that moment or soon after
- Demonstrate you know the audience and can allay their fears
- Be clear and concise; do not leave room for ambiguity.
- Present the benefit to the audience

Additional Thoughts

The Power of Tempo

One of the biggest mistakes people make when speaking is rushing. Rather consider that pausing and taking your time can be highly effective. Simple techniques such as pausing before you speak draws all attention to you. It creates a slight sense of expectation. Using pauses in the middle of an interaction will have the same effect when timed between points.

If you are addressing a group following another presenter, the natural reaction is that we adopt the tempo and theme of the previous speaker. There is a greater impact when we approach it differently, if we want to deliver a slightly different message or address a different topic which needs a distincitve focus.

Imagery & Emotion

Creating an image in the audience's mind is a very powerful emotional connection. We can do this literally by using a visual aid such as a single image on a presentation or we can do it indirectly by describing an image or situation. Both are effective.

In today's visually stimulated society imagery is highly effective. However, if you can describe and create a visual image in someone's mind the main advantage is that they are fully focused on you as the messenger. You can enrich the mental image through the words you use, your emphasis, tempo, depth, and sound. You can increase or reduce the emotional charge. You can calm, excite, or elicit whatever response you want from the audience.

Communication Skills

Listening

Being a good listener is the foundation in order to be a good communicator. No one enjoys communicating with someone who only cares about putting in their two cents and does not take the time to listen to the other person. If you're not a good listener, it's going to be hard to comprehend what you're being asked to do.

Take the time to practice active listening. Active listening involves paying close attention to what the other person is saying, asking clarifying questions, and rephrasing what the person says to ensure understanding ("So, what you're saying is..."). Through active listening, you can better understand what the other person is trying to say and can respond appropriately.

Nonverbal Communication

Your body language, eye contact, hand gestures, and tone of voice all color the message you are trying to convey. A relaxed, open stance (arms open, legs relaxed), and a friendly tone will make you appear approachable and will encourage others to speak openly with you.

Eye contact is also important; you want to look the person in the eye to demonstrate that you are focused on the person and the conversation (however, be sure not to stare at the person, which can make him or her uncomfortable).

Also, pay attention to other people's nonverbal signals while you are talking. Often, nonverbal signals convey how a person is really feeling. For example, if the person is not looking you in the eye, he or she might be uncomfortable or hiding the truth.

Clarity

Good verbal communication means saying just enough – don't talk too much or too little. Try to convey your message in as few words as possible. Say what you want clearly and directly, whether you're speaking to someone in person, on the phone, or via email. If you ramble on, your listener will either tune you out or will be unsure of exactly what you want.

Think about what you want to say before you say it; this will help you to avoid talking excessively and/or confusing your audience.

Demeanor

Through a friendly tone, a personal question, or simply a smile, you will encourage your coworkers to engage in open and honest communication with you. It's important to be nice and polite in all your workplace communications. This is important in both face-to-face and written communication. When you can, personalize your emails to coworkers and/or employees – a quick "I hope you all had a good weekend" at the start of an email can personalize a message and make the recipient feel more appreciated.

Confidence

It is important to be confident in your interactions with others. Confidence shows your coworkers that you believe in what you're saying and will follow through. Exuding confidence can be as simple as making eye contact or using a firm but friendly tone. Avoid making statements that sound like questions. Of course, be careful not to sound arrogant or aggressive. Be sure you are always listening to and empathizing with the other person.

Empathy

Using phrases as simple as "I understand where you are coming from" demonstrate that you have been listening to the other person and respect his or her opinions. Even when you disagree with an employer, coworker, or employee, it is important for you to understand and respect their point of view.

Conclusion

Over the past two years many newly appointed performance directors, as well as up and coming strength coaches have reached out for guidance and advice. The requests have varied from auditing help, technical or personal/career advice, to professional insight. In the majority of cases coaches recognize that the greatest limiting factor is not technical ability or knowledge, rather the soft skills such as leadership, management, conflict resolution, and communication. There's no doubt that with exceptional technical knowledge you can have a good career in this industry. However, your ability to have a long and sustained career will depend on your integrity and ability to master the people skills we need, the ability to help, serve and relate to each other.

Who is Dr. Fergus Connolly?

Dr. Fergus Connolly is one of the world's leading experts in team sports and human performance. He is the only coach to have worked full-time in every major league around the world. Fergus partners with teams at the highest levels integrating best practices in all areas of performance.

His highly acclaimed book 'Game Changer - The Art of Sports Science' is the first blueprint for coaches to present a holistic philosophy for winning in all team sports.

His second best seller '59 Lessons: Working with the World's Greatest Coaches, Athletes, & Special Forces' reveals the secrets learned first-hand from working with the world's greatest winners.

Fergus has served as director of elite performance for the San Francisco 49ers, sports science director with the Welsh Rugby Union, and performance director and director of football operations for University of Michigan Football. He has mentored and advised coaches, support staff, and players in the NBA, MLB, NHL, Australian Rules Football, and international cricket. Fergus has also trained world boxing champions and advises elite military units and companies across the globe.

He is a keynote speaker and consultant to high performing organizations around the world.

Learn more at fergusconnolly.com

4

Mental Resilience Training

Assorted Thoughts and Concepts of Current Trends

Dan A. Pfaff

Pfaff Sports Consultancy

A common term of discussion evident in many performance settings these days seems to be "mental toughness" or "mental skills" training. Sport-specific coaches and especially S&C coaches are often tasked with developing athlete skills or abilities in this realm. Often there is not much clarity on the difference or even the definition of the two terms. There also seems to be a trend in sport circles for leadership to look at military and or special forces work in this area of interest. Somehow a component of this work, namely putting an athlete in extreme physical duress, has seemingly co-opted the approach to enhancing this quality.

Mental resilience training is much more nuanced and complex than merely grinding folks into submission, team building exercises, gut checks screaming top-down leadership, and emotional intimidation techniques.

My network has numerous individuals working with special forces operators, SWAT teams, rapid assault teams, etc. and in every case, they report a layered CBT/Positive Psychology approach being utilized in developing mental skills or resilience under fire so to speak.

The following is a synopsis and consolidation of current work being done by U.S. Military researchers who are working to aid our troops, specifically Special Forces groups doing multiple tours of duty in very dangerous confines. Three authors collaborated on a noteworthy paper found in the journal *American Psychologist*, January 2011. The title of the work is "Master Resilience Training in the U.S. Army." The contributors are Karen J. Reivich, Martin Seligman and Sharon McBride.

The items discussed within this article are also supported by other worldwide research projects undertaken by similar factions involved in extreme warfare situations and crisis encounters. Sport finds its roots and origins in military preparation since recorded history. It is a solid place to do research and possibly transfer lessons and philosophies of operational management theory.

Current troop education matters in this area of interest center around three foundational areas. The first leg is termed "preparation components" which essentially means teaching the fundamentals of resilience. The second domain is described as "sustainment components" and it covers the deployment cycle of the troops. The last element is referred to as "enhancement component" which focuses on personal and professional skills that maximize individual performance. For sporting purposes, I believe this can be termed: preseason, in-season and post-season.

Resilience training is defined by this group as a set of processes that enables good outcomes in spite of serious threats. This trait would obviously be a valuable tool at major championship or critical games. They further define this work as the ability to persist in the face of challenges and to bounce back from adversity.

Protective factors that contribute to resiliency include optimism, effective problem solving, faith, sense of meaning, self-efficacy, flexibility, impulse control, empathy, close relationships and spirituality. The researchers coded and analyzed hundreds of trait personality factors and the above attributes were the most statistically significant and had the greatest reliability in successive tour duty debriefs.

We have extensive data on the use of these components, and they can serve as a grid for self-analysis on periodically designed reflection periods whether it is at the end of a training cycle, after a series of competitions or end of the year debriefs.

Additional research done in the related areas of Positive Psychology included the supplemental metrics of emotional awareness and general self-regulation. These measures in turn led the clinicians to the exploration of signature strengths, cultivating gratitude, and active constructive responding. Again, these items should be found on one's athletic analysis tool grid.

Albert Ellis proposed "adversity/belief/consequence" models decades ago and the takeaway for us is that beliefs about events drive one's emotions and behaviors. To I would assert that it is imperative to monitor beliefs that we hold and work hard at evaluating the accuracy of these beliefs. Often times we need the outside counsel of friends, teammates, experts, and advisors to do this in a timely and honestly fashion.

When people drift off course they are frequently trapped in the vortex of the dysfunctional loop of behavior and do not always entertain rational thought schemes. This can occur at any stage of the practice or game so relying merely on physical duress schemes does little to address the timing and environment of the issue being encountered. Analyzing self-talk habits, obsessive thought patterns and trends of both metrics can be critical determinants in strategy for improved coping skills.

A key tenet in the Ellis model is "explanatory style," which describes how individuals explain both positive and negative events in their lives. Pessimists attribute causes of negative events to permanent, uncontrollable, and pervasive factors. Interesting to note on this topic is that depressed people are more pessimistic than their peers; also, folks with pessimistic tendencies are at greater risk for depression. We most likely do not belong to of either class, but we are burdened at times of these states; note how they feed one another.

Optimists tend to attribute the causes of negative events to temporary, changeable and specific factors. Our job is to learn how to detect inaccurate thoughts generated by faulty explanatory styles or states, evaluate the accuracy of those thoughts, and to reattribute those thoughts to more accurate causal beliefs.

To date, there have been over twenty studies done to evaluate the effectiveness of the program and the metrics just discussed. Field reviews combined with laboratory analysis reveal that these tools reduce anxiety, depression, adjustment disorders, and conduct problems. In a related sidebar, it is my belief that some athletes suffer from a form of post-traumatic stress disorder (PTSD) after major competitions and/or seasons. PTSD is labelled as a "nasty combination of depressive and anxiety symptoms." The crux here is that if you currently have or have dealt with these behavioral factors in the past, then it is imperative that you seek help in dealing with these factors for they may cycle into dormant states at times only to reignite in the crucible of extreme stress.

Theme loops for elite athlete performance based on our research and data collection are:

7. Adversity>beliefs>consequences>emotion>behaviors
8. Accurate causal beliefs>identify true causes of fear>identify distractions>identify negative emotion sources
9. Inaccurate thoughts can be generated solely by explanatory style
10. Soldiers schooled in these concepts become excellent in teaching and leading with these tools.

Module 1: Teaching Resilience to Athletes

- Self-awareness: identifying one's thoughts, emotions and behaviors; identify patterns in each that are counterproductive.
- Self-regulation: the ability to regulate impulses, thinking, emotions, and behaviors to achieve goals as well as the willingness and ability to express emotions.
- Optimism: noticing the goodness in self and others; identifying what is controllable, remaining wedded to reality and challenging counterproductive beliefs.
- Mental agility: thinking flexibly and accurately, perspective taking and willingness to try new strategies; contingency skills are critical in open-chain sporting events.
- Character strengths: identifying the top strengths in oneself and others, relying on one's strengths to overcome challenges and meet goals and cultivating a strength approach in one's squad or unit.
- Connection: building strong relationships through positive and effective communication, empathy, willingness to ask for help, and disposition to offer help.

Module 2: Elite Athlete Development, Building Mental Toughness

ABC model

A = activating event

B = beliefs

C = consequences of thoughts

One must identify thoughts that are triggered by certain activating events. This can range from components in training to specific occurrences during competition. It is suggested that you search through many varied of scenarios that you will encounter this season whether it be in the arena, on the practice track, in life 101, or the daily walk of life. It is very important to realize that not only professional but personal activating events must be explored. The goal here is to separate the activating events from what you say to yourself in the heat of the moment and the emotions/behaviors these thoughts generate. In my experience, athletes who can identify problematic self-talk and remedy the moment are the ones who consistently find themselves on the podium.

We must constantly be on the lookout for thought patterns that are driving adaptive outcomes and patterns that are driving counterproductive outcomes. A goal for this module is that one can distinguish activating events, thoughts and consequences. Realize that chronic strategies actually change biochemistry and at a certain point in that shift, direct mental input is futile.

Module 3: Elite Athlete Experiences, Explanatory Styles and Thinking Traps

Explanatory styles and other patterns of thinking can either increase technical efficiencies, output, and mental health measures or diminish them; there is no middle ground here. It is important to learn about emotional and behavioral consequences for each thinking style you employ, especially the ones under stressful encounters. It is also important to monitor key word triggers that flip us into possible negative loops.

Years ago, I worked with a brilliant cognitive behavior therapist from Spain and she coined a term that has stuck with me for years and has driven a good part of my self-reflective moments. That term was "Thinking Traps." Thinking traps often include jumping to conclusions on scant logical evidence. A common example of this is over generalization and judging one's personal worth, motivation and/or ability on the basis of a single episode. Unfortunately, many of these landmines were established early in our lives, often times away from sport, but we learn to carry them into the arena. As with any behavior, if we constantly default to these modes they become automated and deeply engrained.

Exploration of thinking traps should result in one identifying critical information that is classically missed when trapped in that particular mindset. It is imperative that over time the athletes can identify their specific thinking patterns and have practiced using specific questions once noted that they are within the trap to broaden the information being processed. As with any of the aforementioned topics in this paper, seeking expert advice and direction is critical and these items of discussion are being exposed to improve discussions, seeking of care, and discriminating care providers.

Module 4: Going Deeper; Icebergs or Deeply Held Beliefs

I can handle whatever comes my way. Asking for help is a sign of weakness. I can always turn it on when I need to. People should be treated with dignity and respect. We are all equal. We should strive for forgiveness and mercy. The previous sentences in this paragraph are classic phrases and common core values for many elite athletes, HOWEVER....

Can these icebergs drive out-of-proportion emotions, which in turn switch on faulty reactions, in the field of play? It is recommended by these experts in this study of Special Forces soldiers to ask the following questions about any and all of your core beliefs and values:

1. Is this iceberg still meaningful to you today?
2. Is this iceberg accurate in the given situation?
3. Is this iceberg overly rigid?
4. Is this iceberg truly useful in the moment of fire?

Module 5: The Battery System for Development, Energy Management

Most athletes have spent time in this realm via mainstream sports psychology advices. The management of energy through meditation, controlled breathing exercises, and progressive muscle relaxation techniques are all proven methods for managing energy and arousal levels. The problem is practice. As with any other component of training and meet management skills, it must be done systematically and regularly. It will not be an aid if you treat these items as if they are a cafeteria, picking some on certain days or periods of the year.

Another area found in this sub-header is the need for rejuvenation in order to maintain resilience. These may include prayer, alternative forms of exercise, diet and supplementation, types of physiotherapy, sleep, and laughter. As mentioned above, they only work if integrated, planned and utilized in a designed method.

Problem Solving

Great athletes enjoy mental puzzles, a trait which separates them from the average. We spend a great deal of our day dealing with problems and solutions, both long term and immediate. It is very easy to get trapped in this process and some folks just seem addicted to entertaining problems. Dealing with sub-viruses when sorting through our laundry list of issues each day is especially difficult. One of the leading sub-viruses with which we often wrestle is what we term "conformational bias", defined by the authors as "the tendency to search for or interpret information in a way that confirms what one already believes." This flaw is rampant in scientific studies and it sadly drives world functions including economic principles and military strategies, so it is no surprise to me that it is epidemic in athlete circles.

I think this is one of the most damaging of all character traits that we have in many of our current squads. It often requires outside counsel to realize this in most cases. ThereforeI recommend strongly that you explore patterns of thinking that hinder an accurate appraisal of a problem, learn to use specific questions to identify factors previously missed that contribute to bias, and that you constantly monitor actions and beliefs for conformational bias every day.

Minimizing Catastrophic Thinking

We all fall victim to this loop at various stages of our careers and lives, and it can be left unabated, this thinking can be a fatal trait. It is defined as ruminating about irrational worst-case outcomes. In the sports arena this obstacle can radically drive up anxiety and paralyze action. The researchers propose here that one should capture the catastrophic thoughts, generate a best-case possibility to ponder and then identify most likely outcomes. Once outcomes are stated or locked in, one should then develop coping strategies for each scenario. Contingency planning (positive) must be a practiced skill.

Catastrophic planning is a virus easily caught and feeds itself sub-consciously, spreading throughout a team in an instant.

Fighting Back Against Counterproductive Thoughts in "REAL TIME"

A multitude of research in the literature exists on this topic so I will briefly touch upon the basics of this aspect. One must have a practiced and concrete game plan to conquer negative or non-productive thoughts in the heat of battle. Reduced confidence and halfhearted engagement will escalate unless one learns to reduce "mental chatter." When I see athletes "mail in" performances with less than driven efforts, I know that this realm is the problem. Cracking the code is not easy.

There are three main antidotes to "mental chatter" and they involve strategies based on evidence, optimism, and perspective. The triad they attack are minimizing, rationalizing, and denial. FEAR is often an acronym for false evidence appearing real....... and this is the source of many of these start-up thoughts.

Leading schools of thought on this topic ask that we, by taking a one time/one circumstance attitude, claim ownership of the situation and always take appropriate responsibility for all actions.

Challenging counterproductive thoughts is not about replacing every negative thought with a positive one. Rather, it is a STOP GAP technique that enables one to focus the present rather than placing oneself or others at greater risk because of distracting thoughts. People who can stay in the NOW are at a huge advantage here. Folks who project into the future or live in the past are in peril.

There is a time and place to discuss worries and persistent negative thoughts as often there is something to be learned from them. The theme of negative thoughts almost always is related to iceberg beliefs; so yes, we need to dissect them but not in the heat of battle.

Cultivating Gratitude

The research on gratitude indicates that individuals who habitually acknowledge and express gratitude derive health benefits, sleep benefits, and relationship benefits. I believe this is a truly fruitful return on investment (ROI). It is a habit that takes practice. Even on the worst of days, there are things we can be grateful for as long as we look hard enough or clear away the wreckage in our minds. If you can't find things to appreciate, ask a trusted friend or advisor. For those lacking a daily gratitude list, it might be a good idea to build one into your training diary. Guys on their fourth tour of duty in Afghanistan can do this, so surely, we can do the same.

Identifying Character Strengths

Learning to identify character strengths in yourself, your opponents, your training mates, and your support staff is a key factor in mental preparedness under fire. In U.S. Army parlance: BE, KNOW, DO! Great athletes are leaders. In order to be a leader, one must know what one must BE. The values and attributes that shape character are foundational. In military circles these revolve around loyalty, duty, respect, selfless service, honor, integrity, and personal courage. Quite a worthy list to use for a daily check-up.

There are multitudes of on-line surveys for leadership and character attributes. Research them. We have excellent resources on site for work in this area. Use it. I think it is key to study these character factors in your opponents and especially within your support network. Look for areas that are common, search for areas where you fall short, aspire to acquire greater depth and breadth of these qualities. By knowing the strengths of others, you develop contingency plans without even realizing it. By having strength focus on others, we can build stronger connections and greater faith that on gameday will weather the storm.

With the big game close at hand, it may be well worth the exercise of focusing on using strengths (individual and support team) to overcome challenges both in imagery work and in real time occurrences which result in success. It is also important to journal past "strengths in challenge" and establish a long list of overcoming successes.

Strengthening Relationships

Relationships come in many forms and shapes. No man can truly be an island. We are meant to be social beings and by being a part of a training group, utilizing support service staff and living life 101, we have to evolve relationships daily. In my experience, catastrophic failures at Olympic Games are almost always rooted in relationship issues. Resilience training experts for Special Forces members suggest that three key skill sets are needed to be consistently bold and effective when involved in ongoing relationships. They include; active constructive responding, praise, and effective communication styles. We have to acquire skill sets that help in building relationships and that challenge beliefs that interfere with positive communication. When an individual responds actively and constructively (as opposed to passively and destructively) to someone sharing a positive experience, better relationships ensue.

1. There are four styles of relationship responding: active constructive (authentic, enthusiastic support), passive constructive (understated support), passive destructive (ignoring or partial acknowledgement of the event), and active destructive (pointing out negative aspects of the event). We need to not only listen and grid the conversations we have with others but also look at tone of voice, body language, and the emotions conveyed. It is helpful also to explore ways that trip us into improper responding and discover how to use our signature strengths to respond constructively and actively when under fire.

2. Praise can be a fine art form in this day of haste and facade living. Juman nature craves to be noticed for positive actions. Coaches, support staff, teammates, family, agents, sponsors, etc. all desire praise, which can make life much more joyful and less stressful if you study this response technique. Learning to emphasize a praise concept that points out a specific strategy, effort or skill that contributed to a good outcome as opposed to more general praise such as the one-size-fits-all term of "Good Job!!" can and will make a huge difference in communication.

3. Effective praise expresses the understanding that you were truly watching and listening, that you took time to identify how the person brought on positive action, and that praise was authentic.
4. In learning how to use assertive communication techniques one must explore deeply held beliefs and core values (icebergs) that promote one style of communication over another. The researchers in these studies present a five-step model to improve assertive communication.

- Identifying and working to understand the situation

- Movement towards an acceptable change

- Listing benefits to the situation and the relationship when the change is implemented

- Describing the situation objectively and accurately

- Expressing concerns

- Asking the other person for his or her perspective, monitoring while in discussion body language, voice tone, pace of speech and emotions conveyed.

If these metrics do not line up to what you are hearing, then one needs to present these notices in the conversation or at another time. Also important is to track responses and conversations looking for ways that you typically respond and to identify factors that make it challenging for you to respond actively and constructively. Using signature strengths can unravel the most lost conversation in the world.

Sustaining Mental Resiliency

In Special Forces training a lot of time and work is spent on MRT for pre-deployment and post-deployment situations. In sport, I think we can transfer these to pre-meet and post-meet scenarios. Knowing what to expect in terms of psychological demands and reactions during the entire competition is critical. Good contingency plans involve all possible outcomes and occurrences. Those who fail to review in depth and from all angles limit performance.

Enhanced MRT Components

These are the skill sets so often taught in sport psychology, but they often are "cart before the horse" if the previous modules have not been thoroughly considered, worked on, tested, and refined. Some of the more recognizable skills are:

1. Mental skills foundations: understanding the nature of high performance, understanding the relationship between training and trusting mindsets, and identifying the connection between thoughts, emotions, physiological states and performance.

2. Building confidence: this involves learning effective ways to create energy, optimism and enthusiasm.

3. Goal setting: a systematic process of identifying personal aims and ambitions and tangible action plans that "bolster a commitment to pursue and achieve excellence."

4. Attentional control: the concentration demands associated with all facets of training and competing; also referred to as FOCUS and the world's best are experts at switching from broad to narrow, external to internal and they know where to be at any given moment on the key day, key moment.

5. Energy management: acquiring practical skills used to activate, sustain and restore optimal levels of energy while minimizing the negative effects of stressors.

6. Imagery: involves learning ways to create or recreate successful experiences that can enhance aspects of performance including preparing, performing, and recovering.

7. I have found that far too many do this from a limited perspective. Seeing yourself in all sorts of positions, weather, emotions, conflicts, and attacks from multiple sources is imperative when practicing this aspect.

In conclusion, the hope here is that these somewhat random modules will allow you to systematically review where you sit on key mental resiliency metrics.

Again, these skills involve 12 core blocks or thoughts discussed in this paper:

1. ABC
2. Thinking traps
3. Icebergs
4. Energy management
5. Problem solving
6. "Put it in perspective"
7. Real time resilience
8. Identifying strengths in self and others
9. Using strengths in challenges
10. Assertive communication
11. Active constructive responding and praise
12. "Hunt the good stuff"

Who is Dan Pfaff?

Internationally experienced and recognized educator/coach with forty-five years of multifaceted work. Background in directorships of international training centers, coaching staff development, Division I intercollegiate track and field as a head coach, as well as numerous assistant coaching and teaching positions.

Extensive experience as a lecturer and curriculum designer for international, national, regional, state and community level sports theory symposia and schools. Highly qualified leader with demonstrated abilities in integrated support team management, coach and support staff development/mentoring, and community relations. Actively involved with consulting services to a number of professional teams, support staffs and individual athletes in a variety of sports both domestically and internationally. Internationally recognized as a high-performance center director having served domestically and internationally.

Performance Overview:

Tutored fifty-three Olympians (ten medalists), fifty-eight World Championship competitors (eleven medalists), and five world record holders. Directed athletes to fifty-seven national records. This includes two Paralympic Gold medalists and two Paralympic World Records.

Coached at 10 Olympic Summer Games and served on five Olympic Games coaching staffs (five countries) and ten World Championships staffs (six countries).

Lectured in thirty-seven countries and published in over twenty countries.

Appointed coaching education curriculum chair for both the United States Track and Field Coaches Education Schools and the NACAC Caribbean Basin Project. Lead instructor for each organization at the Level I, II, and III schools.

Provided consultancy to players and teams in the NFL, MLB, NHL, PGA, Canadian Winter Olympic Programs, WTA, AFL and European Soccer Leagues.

Coached twenty-nine NCAA individual national champions and one hundred fifty All-Americans.

Lead staff member on teams that have won seventeen NCAA National Team Championships (fifteen women, two men).

5

Summation of Force
The Key to Rotational Power Development

Jeff Moyer and Brian Mathews

Dynamic Correspondence

Working with rotational sport athletes can be a fun challenge (depending on your idea of fun). However, finding what transfers to improving an athlete's throwing / hitting power isn't as easy as one thinks. Often times as strength coaches we assume that if we lift X then we will see Y improvement in athletic performance. Unfortunately, when improving throwing/hitting ability, we can't simply hope to slap an extra 30 pounds on an athlete's bench press and then assume corresponding results. If that were the case, Brian Shaw or Hafthor Bjornson would be lining up under center for the Pats while Tom Brady was wearing a headset and sending in signals from the sideline.

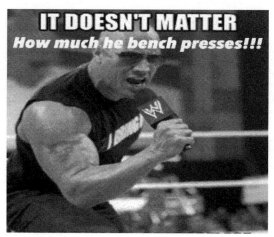

This is not to say that a quarterback doesn't need to bench press! What we *are* saying is that there is a law of diminishing returns with the transference of bench pressing and throwing power.

Clearly, exclusively general practices are not the answer to make an athlete rotationally robust. A more specific means of supplementing throws and hits exists in medicine ball training. Using this tool to bolster throwing and hitting has become a popular means of training rotational power. Popularity can be good, as more athletes and trainers can be exposed to these ideas. However, popularity can also dilute the underlying reasons to do an exercise is initially intended. The HOW in the selection and performance of these exercises is truly the difference between actually improving transverse force development and general busy work. For young athletes, typically any basic throw will transfer. Yet with the higher training ages, these throws must start to resemble the joint actions that we see in the athlete's sport. Having a proper understanding of biomechanics of throwing / hitting will help bridge the gap between general exercises and specialized efforts.

Often times you will hear coaches say things such "that kid is an arm thrower", or "They need to get their hips into it more." They aren't necessarily wrong, but explore these thoughts a little more deeply. What those statements even mean? Yes, in order to throw, you must use your arm, and of course you need to get your hips into throwing. But how?!

The fact that the lower body is the main contributor of force isn't a new idea. However, if force is developed from the lower body, then how is the force transferred to the arm / hand? This is usually left out of an explanation of HOW force is generated from the lower body and transferred into arms / hands. Additionally, what muscles are involved, how they are involved, what joint actions occur, and what is the sequencing of these actions?

We believe that understanding the muscles involved, how they are involved, the joint actions that occur and their sequencing will allow "strength and conditioning coaches" to better select exercises and program their training so as to transfer into better throwing / hitting / rotational movements on the field.

Summation of Forces:

In physics, a summation of force is all body parts acting sequentially: the strongest and lowest body parts around the center of gravity move first, followed by the weaker, lighter, and faster extremities. This is also known as sequential acceleration and results in successive force summation.

Force summation has to do with several things: total number of body parts, the order in which it is produced, the timing of their actions, the velocity and sum of all of the force. So, for example, in basic math $1+1+1+1+1 = 5$. The 5 is the total sum, while each individual "1" is a part that helps make up the total.

In every type of rotational movement, there should be a summation of forces. The way that I describe this to my athletes is to think about a link of chain vs a standard stick. The link is connected from one rung to the next. The premise behind summation of force captures that idea nicely: Legs + Trunk + Shoulders + Arm + Wrist = Throw

With a stick we would see no discernible break in the different actions. It would look something like this:

> Arm - legs - trunk - shoulders - wrist = throw

It is the summation of forces from the joint actions that follow a specific progression that culminates in maximum force. To quote Dr. Michael Yessis:

"Each joint action must occur in sequence so that the force generated by one action can then be transferred to the next action. When the force generated from one joint action is transferred to the next joint, such as the legs to the hips to the shoulders to the arm to the wrist... it allows for the culmination of maximum force (and speed)." (1)

Therefore, the most efficient and powerful actions occur when the force from the preceding joint is added to the next joint action. For this to occur, all of the joint actions cannot occur simultaneously: they must occur in a sequence with some overlapping between them if you are to generate maximum force.

Muscles and Sequence of Actions:

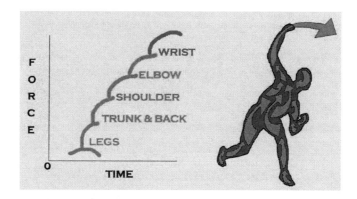

When seeking to increasing rotational power, understanding that force is generated from the lower body is only part of the equation. Studies on athletes involved in rotational sports such as boxing, baseball (2), softball, football, tennis, and volleyball show similar lower body trunk mechanics and have shown for years how important the lower body is for force generation. The understanding of how the force is transferred into the throw / hit that will make a huge difference towards the practical application for strength and conditioning coaches.

In order to obtain force from the legs into the throw / hit, you must start with a weight shift onto the front leg. As noted in the studies by Filmonov (3), the weight shift (*"push-*

off leg extension") is the main source of force production. It is important to get the hips in motion in order to overcome inertia, get the body in motion, and direct the forces towards your target. The joint actions are right hip joint abduction with hip internal rotation.

Once the weight has been shifted onto the front leg, it is now the base of support and the left hip (for a righthanded thrower/hitter) becomes the axis of rotation for the pelvis and the shoulder girdle. Holding the front leg stiff is essential (isometric contraction), so that the weight shift can be transferred to the hip and trunk. That front leg stiffness is a major factor in transferring power. The greater the front leg sinks, the more the force from the weight shift will be lost. As the hips rotate forward around the left hip, the shoulders must still be side-facing. This creates a separation between the hips and the shoulders. The separation causes an eccentric contraction in the right external and the left internal oblique muscles while the shoulders are still facing the side position. The forward hip rotation prepares for a forceful rotation of the shoulders. Once the hips decelerate into the front facing position, they contract isometrically, creating a firm base for the obliques to contract and rotate the shoulders. This action produces, mechanically, a long force arm. As the hips decelerate, the shoulders begin to rotate due to a concentric contraction of the right and left obliques. (4)

"The lag between pelvis rotation and upper trunk rotation is critical for generating energy from the trunk that is passed along to the throwing arm. Without proper timing of pelvis and upper trunk rotation, the athlete may have low-ball speed and/or excessive loads in the shoulder and elbow". (5)

The greater force of the shoulder rotation contributes to creating greater arm speed.

The shoulder / arm / wrist action varies depending on the sport and the position. For a field player in baseball this will look different than for a pitcher, which looks a bit different than a quarterback, which is different for a closed stance forehand & backhand in tennis. In sports such as baseball and softball, once the weight has shifted and the hip rotation has occurred, the shoulder rotation then cocks the arm. Once again, this can vary from sport to sport and athlete to athlete. Quarterbacks generally want a quicker release, while baseball and softball athletes generally want power. So, cocking the arm sooner can help with creating more power. This is where the term "arm thrower" originates. An athlete that cocks their arm too soon into the motion and then tries to generate their power with their arm.

Practical:

The first action that occurs in throwing / hitting is getting the hips in motion; shifting the weight from the back leg onto the front. As noted in the studies done by Filmonov (6), the weight shift (*"push-off leg extension"*) is the main source of force production. A general-specific exercise to strengthen this joint action is performing hip ab-duction.

Once the weight has been shifted, hip rotation occurs around the front leg while keeping the shoulders side facing. This separation is important in order to create a powerful "rubber band" affect with stretching of the obliques. The more separation there is between the hips and shoulders, the stronger the contraction of the obliques, which then whips the shoulders around. Reverse Trunk Twists are a great exercise to create flexibility between the hips and shoulders as well as strength in a full range of motion.

The Russian Twist is an exercise that often times is overlooked for development of the oblique muscles. Performed properly on a Glute-Ham-Back machine will allow for a full range of motion of the obliques and is done against the direct pull of gravity. Russian Twists have been modified throughout the years to be performed in a seated position to make this easier. Executing the exercise this way shortens up the ROM, and can allow for spine flexion, which combined with rotation can lead to injury.

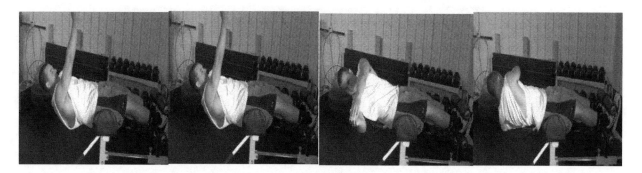

As stated earlier, rotational med-ball throws are a great way to develop rotational speed, power, and strength. There are many different variants of med ball throws that can be used in the programming for rotational sport athletes ranging from general to specialized. The use of specialized exercises is to improve the athlete's physical abilities as related to technique. Specialized exercises can be single joint as well as multi-joint exercises. In order to make med-ball throws specialized, the lower-body and torso must duplicate how it is used in throwing a punch. The overload of the med ball must be such that it does not allow for mechanics over the lower body and torso to change.

Most often rotational med-ball throws are performed with a simultaneous weight shift, rotation of the hips and shoulders. In order to make it more specialized there must be a sequencing of the joint actions. Otherwise it is best to use these general med-ball throws with lower level athletes, and/or in the general phase of training.

Figure 1.   Figure 2.   Figure 3.   Figure 4.

1. Figure 1 shows a side-facing athlete to his target

2. Figure 2 shows the athlete shifting his weight onto his front leg by hip joint abduction

3. Figure 3 shows the athlete performing hip joint rotation.

   - The axis of his rotation is in his left hip
   - His shoulders remain side-facing as his hips reach full rotation

4. Figure 4 shows the athlete then coming around with his shoulders as he releases the ball

Performing rotational exercises with the hips and ribs locked together is great for GENERAL rotational development. However, in order to have true transfer, the hips and shoulders must have separation. Understanding the joint and muscle actions of throwing and hitting and how certain exercises can impact these movements is a major piece in truly enhancing performance. If fully grasped and programmed effectively, you can be sure to see healthier, happier and improved trainees. We hope that the concepts covered in this text will not only aid with the science behind the methods but also offer some real-world practical exercises you can guide your athletes to perform today.

REFERENCES

1. Michael Yessis. Explosive Tennis.

2. Picture http://biomechanics-gridiron-throw.blogspot.com

3. Fleisig. *Biomechanics of Baseball Pitching: Implications for Injury and Performance.* American Sports Medicine Institute, Birmingham, AL, USA. XXVIII International Symposium of Biomechanics in Sports

4. Filimonov. Means of Increasing Strength of the Punch. NSCA Journal. Vol 7, #6

5. Yessis. Sports Performance Series: Throwing a Football. NSCA Journal. Feb-Mar 1984

6. Filimonov. Means of Increasing Strength of the Punch. NSCA Journal. Vol 7, #6

Who is Brian Matthews?

Having worked with hundreds of local athletes in the 518 since 2008 Brian has a passion for making local athletes the best they can be. A hybrid physical prep/strength/speed/mobility coach Brian has written for several fitness publications including Muscle & Fitness and stack.com. He has worked with ability levels from youth to the professional ranks. His philosophy is simple (and heavily influenced by World Class coach Henk Kraaijenhof) "Find the right program for your athlete, not the right athlete for your program! Brian can be reached at brian@accelerate-athletics.com.

Who is Jeff Moyer?

Jeff Moyer is the owner of Dynamic Correspondence Sports Training, whose motto is, "We Build Better Athletes." At DC Sports Training, athletes work on the physical, mental and visual aspects to the sports. Their goal is to deliver the athletes of the greater Pittsburgh area the highest, most efficient results year after year of training with us. We will exhaust our means in order for our athletes to achieve the highest results, and to create a system model that will develop our athletes both physically and intellectually. Education must be the road to which will help us set this standard. Our results will be the vehicle which to drive us.

Jeff graduated in 2004 from Hartwick College where he was a two-sport athlete (Football & Track & Field). Jeff has been a sport coach (Basketball & Football) at the youth, JV, Varsity and College level for football for over 10years. Jeff has been in the strength in conditioning industry for over a decade, having worked in the medical, private, team, high school and collegiate settings, training clients from youth development, to rehabilitation and sport performance.

Jeff has a relentless passion for all thing's physical preparation. His pedagogy is heavily influenced by Eastern Bloc sport science, while apprenticing under Dr. Michael Yessis and Yosef Johnson of Ultimate Athlete Concepts. Jeff has also been fortunate enough to extensively study with and work with Dr. Natalia Verkhoshansky, Mike Woicik of the Dallas Cowboys, Louie Simmons of Westside Barbell, and Fellowship under Dave Tate of EliteFTS.

6

Culture Club: A Story of Struggle and Growth in High Performance Sport

Devan McConnell

Head of Hockey Performance and Sport Science

UMass Lowell

There is something that defines all great organizations. Something that connects the dots, ties everything together, secures the last piece of the puzzle. That something is present across disciplines, be it business, sport, religion, education, etc. It isn't just talent. Talent alone is too simplistic and superficial an answer for the multifaceted complexities of organizational success. Long is the list of talented teams who have failed to reach the pinnacle of their universe. As was noted in the book, *Legacy* by James Kerr (2013), "A collection of talented individuals without personal discipline will ultimately and inevitably fail. Character triumphs over talent."

Many teams are constructed as if they were an all-star contingent. It consists of uber-talented individuals thrown together with the hopes that their collective skill level will overcome their collective egos and other shortfalls. Unfortunately, success in team sport rarely comes simply to the most talented collection of DNAs. Much more is necessary on the road to accomplishment. No, while talent is surely requisite, in and of itself, it is not enough. Roles must be played. Chemistry must be created…but what is the "it" that ties talent to a larger purpose?

Money? More than a few big spenders have come and gone with little to show for their deep pockets besides regret and humiliation. Money, often times, can buy you the talent. It can buy you the tools and the toys. Money and resources are crucial to the overall effort, but money alone cannot create the connection that is so desired and so sought after in all high-performance organizations. Money is akin to the false grail in Indiana Jones and the Last Crusade… "*He chose…poorly.*" Without question, resources matter. They may help you succeed but resources are not the key. Without "it," money just leads an organization astray.

Is it simply knowledge? Certainly knowledge, intelligence, and aptitude matter, as do resources and talent, but not by themselves. In our current sports performance climate, many understand the technicalities, but there are few that can apply, and even rarer are those who can tie the technical know-how and simplistic application to the greater whole. The land of the keyboard warrior has never been so vast. Social media has been a boon to well-meaning and well-intentioned professionals. An ever expanding educational and networking landscape has aided many legitimate careers in the recent decade. But like so much else in our society, there is an ugly, hidden plague lurking behind computer screens. Knowledge is and should be a never-ending quest. The desire to improve, to search out what is unknown is a hallmark of the best professionals in the performance fields. But the dark side of social media and the ever expanding and demanding search for "knowledge," especially without application and experience, is an intensifying problem.

So, what is...."it"? What is that certain "something" that should constitute the ground floor of our high-performance setting?

Culture.

What exactly is, culture? It is a fairly vague term. Depending on the context, culture can have slightly different meanings. Organizational culture. Societal culture. Religious culture. The culture of a locker room. The culture of a department. What all of these have in common is that "culture" represents a code of conduct that all parties within the group agree to and abide by. The recent paper, "Building a High-Performance Model for Sport" (Turner, et. al, 2018) defines culture this way: "Culture describes the ideas, customs, and social behaviors of a community, and may simply be described as "the way we do things around here".

Any group or team will have a culture…it is part of what makes a collection of individuals into a team in the first place. The strength of that culture is the question. More specifically, what will have the most influence on all the extraneous details that we all attempt to institute in search of improvement and success? When the culture of an organization is weak, the "code" can be broken with little to no repercussions. It isn't that the individual or the group doesn't understand what is right and what is not…it's that they don't view that particular "thing" as important enough to hold firm to the standards set forth. A weak culture is still a culture, it's just one that doesn't collectively elevate the team, and often has the opposite effect. A weak culture can become insidious, creating an environment that spirals downward and out of control. A rising tide lifts all ships…and a receding tide can have the opposite effect.

This invisible line between what is accepted and what is not, is often referred to as "the standard". Like culture, there is always a standard. Whether or not the standard is held high, and whether or not there are consequences to not upholding said standard, is largely what defines a culture as robust or frail. The standard is always there and how high it's held is what matters most in culture development. This is a huge factor in what makes or breaks a program or an organization, especially over the long term. Aspects of a high-performance model are successful when, ex. sport science integration, is established during a strong foundational culture. Only when the standard is elevated can sport science and performance training flourish. When sport science fails, or leadership doesn't develop, it is often because the culture surrounding and underpinning the program is not strong enough to allow for organic growth, which is a valuable piece of the entire high-performance model.

The standard can be thought of as the framework of a team's culture. It is the decree that defines what is expected within the confines of the team, and what is not acceptable to the collective purpose. High or low standards can be in place, either consciously or unconsciously, and where that line falls is really demarcated by what is allowed. No one claims to have low standards in a high-performance organization, but actions speak louder than words. If a talented athlete is allowed to live up to a different set of standards from the rest of the team, the cumulative standard is ultimately downgraded, and the overarching culture of the group is as well. An empty water bottle left on the floor. The barbells put back on the rack at different heights. A player wearing the wrong shirt. Broken Windows theory…the Slight Edge…Marginal Gains…the "slippery slope." Everything matters. And as one thing goes, so do the rest. The cumulative effect of "doing the right thing" is what ultimately sets the height of the standard, and the foundation of the culture.

Developing great culture should be the ultimate goal of any high-performance organization. But how do you go about building one? Where should you start? There is not a one-size-fits-all model, although there are plenty of examples from sport and business organizations that have built and maintained this ephemeral "great culture" (ex. All Blacks, Apple, Disney, Zappos, San Antonio Spurs). It is what these organizations have in common that I believe are the building blocks of a great organizational culture. Like a collection of great strength and conditioning coaches, it's not the differences between their programs that are the foundation to great training, but the similarities.

These are the aspects we want to identify and study. These are the areas that I believe are the building blocks of great organizational culture.

Accountability.

Great cultures are those in which accountability is front and center. Accountability is a key component of trust, and trust is absolutely imperative for the development of a robust culture. What's more, accountability in these types of organizations does not just come from the top down, but is embraced by the individual, and is dispersed laterally across the group. In teams with great culture, the athletes hold themselves and their teammates accountable to the standards that have been set. The team self-polices. This often manifests in one of several forms, largely based on the identity of the team and the make-up of the players. Some teams consist of leadership groups that take control of any minor issues that may arise. Other teams are less hierarchically structured but more broadly ranging with their constituent's leadership characteristics. In these groups, any player can, and is expected to, hold any other player accountable. Senior to Freshmen and Freshmen to Senior, these types of groups value a more holistic model of leadership and accountability. Either way, when all parties understand the needs and the structure of the group, a player-led culture is born. When this operates effectively, it becomes a key component to the growth of a strong culture.

Trust.

I mentioned this above as a component that comes out of accountability; trust is more than just a byproduct of the process. Trust is a necessary ingredient in organizations with a strong culture. Trust must be present between coaches and players, and vice versa. Athletes must trust that the intentions of the coaches and/or management, even when not personally pleasant, are in the best interests of the organization and its vision. Coaches must trust that the players are fully on board with the same vision, and not simply motivated by individual statistics or accolades. Trust must be present between players, or honesty will never be fully available.

Touch.

Physical contact is something that, as odd as it may sound, tends to be present in organizations and teams with strong culture. Physical contact actually underpins trust. By allowing and embracing touch by way of handshakes, high fives, etc., individuals signal to one another that they trust each other, that they care about one another, and that there is a unifying bond between one another. Teams that are close, which is a key component of a strong culture, embrace physical touch more than others, at least in my experience. In a paper by Kraus, et. al. (2010), they found that "Consistent with hypotheses, early season touch predicted greater performance for individuals as well as teams later in the season."

Communication.

It should be fairly obvious that communication is a key ingredient in strong and successful cultures and organizations. Open lines of dialogue between all parties are strongly intertwined with trust. Communication in strong cultures is not always "positive," but is, more often than not, constructive. The aforementioned ingredients need to be present for this to be the case. Individuals need to trust one another and care about one another if they are going to be comfortable enough and receptive enough to give and receive criticism. The best cultures I've been associated with do not just operate this way from the top down, but from the bottom up, as well as laterally. Teammates "coaching" each other, holding each other accountable, when done right and understood in the proper context, can have powerful cultural implications within an organization and foster a sense of greater purpose for all involved.

Leadership.

One of my favorite lines regarding leadership, which I've heard numerous times, has been originally credited to Don McGannon, a broadcasting industry executive during the formative years of television. He famously said, "Leadership is an action, not a position" (Forbes, 2013). All great organizations and teams have great leadership. This can come in different forms depending on the identity of the group. It could be a single leader who elicits great respect and admiration. It could be a leadership group consisting of various constituents of the team. Additionally, it could be a theme that is present across the group, with everyone playing a role. A combination of all three has, in my experience, produced the strongest display of leadership. A team with several strong and complimentary leaders followed by a larger group consisting of a diverse slice of the team with an understanding that everyone plays a role in leadership is, in my opinion, the optimal team leadership model. In this structure, all players are able and expected to speak up when necessary, do the right thing, lead by example, and support everyone involved in the process.

Unifying Vision.

Ultimately, this may be the most important component of a strong culture. Without a unifying vision, there is no "true north" for all parties to orient themselves. Without a purpose, without a "why", communication is just chatter, touch isn't bonding, leadership won't have direction, and there is nothing to make anyone accountable. Creating a "why" is paramount, and it must be organic. It does no good to have the vision dictated down from atop an ivory tower. This isn't to say management, ownership or some other authoritarian entity doesn't have final say or the ability to mold and direct the vision, but it must be a collaborative approach if it is going to be something truly unifying. Having a purpose behind anything you do is important; a team having a vision for why they do what they do is the foundation of culture building. As Simon Sinek has so famously put it, "People don't buy what you do, they buy why you do it." (*Start with Why*, 2013).

Connection.

Lastly, a bond to something greater than yourself is another hallmark of strong cultures. Believing in a greater purpose or knowing the long history of those that have come before and upheld the organization's standard high, especially during turbulent times, is often associated with a culture that has withstood the test of time. Without this anchor point, it is hard for new members of a group, team, or business to understand the lessons of the past. As Churchill said in 1948, "Those that fail to learn from history are doomed to repeat it." The role of history and a bond to the past is an important centering point for an organization. It allows for consistent onboarding of new employees or teammates by educating and integrating them into the collective "why."

A Framework for Culture

Now that we have discussed some of the key ingredients that are necessary for a strong team culture, I want to provide an example of how we went about trying to influence the culture within our program. One of my favorite lines about the role of a High-Performance Manager came from David Tenney, who at the time was with the Seattle Sounders, but is currently with the Orlando Magic. He said (paraphrasing) that being a High-Performance Manager was like being the captain of an ocean liner. You don't make sudden, abrupt maneuvers. Your goal is to simply ease the vessel slightly to the left or slightly to the right. You can't spin a 300-foot-long ship around on a dime, just like you can't do a 180 with a sports organization overnight. My thought process regarding culture building within an organization that had been very successful over the better part of a decade was similar and was framed by this reference. We weren't trying to make wholesale changes; instead we wanted to take something that was slightly off course and nudge it back towards the direction we needed to go.

Transparency

In the name of transparency, I made my thoughts known at our post season staff debrief, along with how I wanted to address aspects in training. Luckily, all members of the staff were on the same page as far as what was missing with our group the previous year. This wasn't an easy conversation to have, but it was an important one. In *The Culture Code* (2019), Daniel Coyle states; "A winning organization is an environment of personal and professional development, in which each individual takes responsibility and shares ownership." We had to look in the mirror and take responsibility for the change in our team. Our culture had slipped, our leadership hadn't developed the way we had expected, and the team was left rudderless without a "why" behind what they were doing.

We had expected our strong culture to trickle down year to year, without realizing we needed to constantly cultivate it. Our leaders were left unable to take the reins the way we needed them to, because we had neglected to *teach them how* to lead. The players felt no connection with the "why" in which we as coaches believed in because we hadn't communicated it with them well enough. More importantly, we hadn't involved them in the process of discovering and deciding what that "why" was. They felt no ownership to the hollow words that formed our motto. So, what was the plan coming out of this initial discussion? The first step in this process was to open the lines of communication with the team.

The general framework was to spend the next six weeks with teamwork, chemistry, and culture building as the nuts and bolts of our physical training. Alwyn Cosgrove's famous quote, "The psychology trumps physiology everyday", could not have been more apt. This was going to be quite a departure from my comfort zone as a coach. As I mentioned earlier in this chapter, I am a big proponent of sport science. I am also hugely influenced by the line "they don't care how much you know until they know how much you care." This epitomizes my approach as a coach and educator. However, I am very science-driven. Each component of my program has a physiological, biomechanical, and/or bio motor purpose, sometimes to a fault. My strengths are in analytical thinking and relationship building, not motivational speeches or sideline dances. That being said, I certainly would need to take a somewhat different approach this offseason and emphasize a re-build to the foundation that we all felt had cracked. So, what follows is how we addressed our concerns.

Player Involved Discussion

My first step was something that I have done in the past, and I feel is an instrumental tool in the ability to open lines of communication, build trust, and create buy-in. "When players know the coach cares about them as individuals, they will get closer to giving their personal bests." (Wooden, *Pyramid of Success*, 2005). This mindset is instrumental in my philosophy as a coach. "They don't care how much you know, until they know how much you care" forms the cornerstone of my approach. Opening myself up to comment and criticism was not only an attempt to gain valuable insight, but to create a bridge of trust with the players.

I formulated an anonymous survey and emailed it out to all my players. Here were the questions:

1. What can I do better to help you and the team?
2. What do you like about our program?
3. What do you dislike about our program?
4. What would you change if you were me?
5. Are there things that other programs are doing better than us?
6. Any other feedback- positive or negative?
7. What is your "why"? Why do you play hockey?

I encouraged the players to be completely transparent and not hold anything back if they had any critiques. As a result, many of the responses were positive and complimentary, but some were not. Some of the answers were, frankly, hard to read. However, I felt that this was a crucial practice in the process of shifting our culture. If we were going to talk about openness, the ability to reflect and adjust, being accountable to our actions, and being coachable, I felt it necessary to lead by example. Again, sage advice from *The Culture Code* (2019): "...most of us instinctively see vulnerability as a condition to be hidden. But science shows that when it comes to creating cooperation, vulnerability is not a risk but a psychological requirement."

I needed honesty so that I could fully understand their perspective. The survey and subsequent group conversation also led to a lot of teachable moments. When we first got back into training, the entire initial session was devoted to going over each question and addressing many of the responses. I was able to explain the "why" behind a lot of things we do in training and clear up any confusion. Some things we would change based on their feedback, some things we wouldn't. However, the process of discussing these points was what mattered most. The process was being hugely cathartic for all of us after a tough season and the tension that had built around it.

The next step was to perform one-on-one interviews with each player, which is something I routinely do after the season. The talking points for the discussions were:

1. What did you think of how we started the off season regarding our debrief/conversation/accountability tasks?
2. What is your personal goal?
3. What do you want our team values/code to be?
4. Grade yourself in the weight room.
5. Why that grade?
6. What can you improve upon?
7. What do you need from me to assist you?

These conversations, held roughly a week or two later from the start of our post season training, allowed me to get into the weeds a bit more with each player, as well as allow them to ask some things of me. One of the absolutely most interesting findings, one with which I'll discuss later, was the number of players who, when we got to question 7, asked for help *learning how* to become a leader...this was a big "aha" moment for me.

Player Directed Accountability

One of my goals for this approach to the post season period was to encourage a return to a high level of accountability. In fact, this was one of the areas that was brought up in the initial survey that was pretty jarring to hear. In short, I had let the team down by not holding them accountable to the details of everyday training. I had let the standard slip. I had to come to grips with this truth, and it wasn't comfortable. It wasn't major things, as our culture was still plenty strong enough to handle those items. The slip occurred in the small, tedious, day-to-day things that can get lost in the hustle and bustle such as: making sure to change the batteries in the bikes, re-stocking the fridge for smoothies, adjusting the daily warm up more often so it didn't become overly tedious, and most importantly, and most difficult to swallow, bringing energy and positivity when everyone else is down. Now, I could have come up with excuses for all of these. "You guys didn't tell me the batteries died...My other commitments make it tough to get to Costco for smoothies...I'm in a bad mood too after a tough weekend." But these would have been just that...excuses. If I wanted them to be more accountable to the details, I needed to step up and do the same.

With that in mind, and with the next step in the culture development program being to get back to the details of accountability, I split the team up into six groups of 4 players. Each platform in our facility was assigned to a group, chosen by me. In each group, I placed (unbeknownst to them) one player I deemed to be a leader, or at least have some strong leadership characteristics, and then a fairly even split of players by class. What I wanted to create were independent groups that would be able to develop their own autonomy, communication, and structure within the larger team.

The first "assignment," if you will, was to assign each group a responsibility... something their group was in charge of for the duration of the spring. For example, one group was in charge of the set-up of each rack and platform. I let them decide (within reason) how each one would be set up: the organization of the plates, how the accessories were stored, etc. But then, the kicker. That particular group was responsible for all of the racks, each day. At the end of a session, if one of the racks was off in some way, it fell on their shoulders. They could manage this anyway they wanted; they could be solely in charge and self-organize each day, they could enlist the help of others or set up a system with which each group would handle things and they would oversee. I didn't really care how they decided to manage their task, but the responsibility and the consequences would fall on them. Other groups had various tasks in their charge, but all were set up the same way. One group was to handle of all the "data" such as making sure everyone had their heart rate belt on, ensuring everyone filled out their online questionnaire on time each day, and other similar items. Another group was obligated to oversee the bikes, plyo boxes, med balls, and other miscellaneous equipment. All of them had autonomy to come up with their own process, thus creating a sense of ownership.

The last piece of this puzzle was one additional group, the "Leadership Accountability" team. I formed one more team, consisting of the "leader" of each group. Their additional task was to establish the consequence for any indiscretion on which each group had decided upon. I gave them autonomy in this area as well. They were able to choose the punishment, but they also would be the ones doling out whatever that sanction might be. I audited this process, of course. I wanted them to eventually call out one another, respectfully, when they saw something that didn't adhere to the established standards. However, if it was something only I caught, I would inform the Leadership Accountability group of the issue, and they would address it. They chose to establish a consequence of 1-mile on the Assault Bike for everyone on the team, and an additional mile for the group who was in charge of the particular area that was "off."

Two days later, we had our first test.

One player had forgotten to do his subjective wellness survey the previous day, which happened to be an off day. As I mentioned this, I told the team that this was my fault, because I had failed to talk to them about the guidelines for completing this task on off days. I would take the fall this time, but we needed to sort this out, so we were all on the same page moving forward. Immediately, one of the players from the Leadership group raised his hand, and said "Coach, we will all just get on the bike. We should have known. And from here on out, it has to be done by 11:30 on days off." And just like that, everyone got up off the turf without so much as an eye roll or a grumble and headed towards the bikes. There was even a little excitement at the prospect of policing themselves and owning up. This was the exact moment I felt like we were onto something.

Developing Trust

I often talk about a great training culture being similar to a self-cleaning oven. If you've done a good job as a coach, at some point, the team should be able to do what needs to get done without your input. The goal should essentially be to make yourself unnecessary. Of course, this will never be the case, as there is always a detail that can be coached, adjustments that can be made, and progressions that should be implemented. The point is that if you have properly developed systems for training, educated and coached your athletes, and the level of understanding, buy-in, and accountability is high enough, the team should be able to mostly run itself. At least, that is my goal. With this in mind, I wanted to regress things down to their most basic level and build back up from that starting point.

During our first phase of post season training, nearly everything we did was on command. Plyo's and med ball throws, paired together, done on my "Set...go!" Lifts done by tempo, along with the clock, while partners called out the seconds, "three, two, one, UP!" Was this some half-witted attempt to instill military, boot camp rituals on our team? Hardly. While certainly akin to what you might see in a movie depicting a ragtag group of misfits getting whipped into shape at boot camp, I'd never be so brash as to pretend I'm some kind of drill sergeant. It wouldn't give our Armed Forces the respect they deserve, and it's really not my style. However, I did see the value in breaking down our training to this level, if only to introduce the lesson of teaching, of coaching one another, and being able to *be coached* by one another.

One of the major teaching points made over and over during this period was that truly great cultures, in my opinion at least, consist of a group that is comfortable and secure enough to be able to say the hard thing to their teammate, and in turn, be able to hear the hard thing without an emotional reaction. If we wanted to be truly great, we couldn't rely on me or any of the other coaches dictating every detail, day after day. After all, what we were doing in the weight room wasn't rocket science. After a few cues by me, everyone knew and could identify the proper position for something like a single leg box drop. So, if you know how that should look, and you understand that our standard is that we do the small things properly, every time, and the guy next to you isn't doing it correctly...who is the jerk? Him, or you when you don't say anything?

Getting to this point was trickier than I had imagined. What I began to realize was that many of my athletes were very uncomfortable critiquing one another, and many others weren't very good at receiving that information. Whether they were timid in saying something to their friend that might not sound too friendly, or tended to take the coaching personally, especially from a peer, I realized at the heart of this roadblock was a lack of trust. That lack of trust originated from a lack of communication. That is where we came up with one of our first "motto's":

TALK, TOUCH, TRUST.

One of the things that grew organically out of this experiment was the weekly theme. It started early on, at the end of our first week. As we debriefed on the first Friday, I addressed the day, and that week: things we had talked about, what I thought we did well, and areas in which I thought we could improve. From there, I tasked the group to spend some time over the weekend coming up with a theme for the next week. In the context of everything we had been discussing and working on, what should our focus be during the next week? What would next week's "why" be? On Monday, the players returned with the three words that we had discussed the most during the past week. These were the keys to developing trust, which would allow for genuine communication, and ultimately a sense of togetherness and genuine care for one another. TALK. TOUCH. TRUST.

The basic premise was this: we needed to be able to trust each other. Trust that when one person tells another person that they need to improve something, or change something, or do something different, (think literally, one player coaching another player's technique), both parties need to understand that the message was coming from a place of caring; caring for that person, caring for the team, and caring for the standard we were setting. In order for these young men to be able to embrace that message, we had to improve the foundation of trust. We needed to communicate. We needed to talk. Literally, we needed to speak to each other, nearly constantly. We needed to cheer for each other, coach each other, and hear each other. If you see someone do something right, tell them. If you see someone do something wrong, tell them. And understand the end goal is to hold each other accountable, so that we all get better together.

Touch

We also needed to touch each other. That's right. Physically touch each other. If you say these are your brothers, if you say you love each other, if you say you want to see your teammates succeed, then show them. High five when you walk by. Fist bump. Hip Check. Touch in this manner, when done appropriately and between two willing and understanding individuals, is a powerful part of developing trust. In the fantastic study by Kraus, et. al., (2010) mentioned earlier, they found that, amongst NBA players, "Consistent with hypotheses, early season touch predicted greater performance for individuals as well as teams later in the season. Additional analyses confirmed that touch predicted improved performance even after accounting for player status, preseason expectations, and early season performance."

It's why we shake hands when a deal is made, or as congratulations for a job well done, or just to say hello. The physical act of touching is a form of communication. If you went to the car dealer to purchase a used car, and the salesman wouldn't shake your hand before you signed on the line, how would you feel? The first weekly theme of TALK, TOUCH, TRUST helped get the ball really rolling. From that point on, there was energy, chatter, high fives, and the beginning of a self-cleaning oven.

Communication

In the *Talent Code* (2009), written by Daniel Coyle, he tells a story about John Wooden, the great UCLA basketball coach. Coach Wooden had a system. He didn't realize it. He didn't come up with it consciously. But it was there, and it was key to how he coached and taught. The Plus/Minus/Plus (+/-/+) system was how he communicated on the court. When a couple of grad students watched his practices for a year, trying to understand what made him and his teams so great, they uncovered this communication system. Wooden's practices were notoriously fast paced. Very little stoppage, very little discussion, very high efficiency. During the entire session, which was meticulously scripted down to the second, Coach Wooden almost never stopped communicating. However, he spoke in short, direct, pinpoint phrases. You could hardly call them sentences, and over time, a pattern emerged.

$$+ / - / +$$

Do this, not that, do this. Go here, not there, go here. Shoot now, not then, shoot now. +/-/+. Brilliant.

One of the greatest coaches who ever lived had a system for delivering only what was necessary, stripping away any extraneous verbiage that only confused and disoriented. I first learned about this method from Mike Boyle. He wrote about it on his StrengthCoach.com blog in 2011, and the idea stuck with me. It was so simplistic and to the point. I make a concerted effort to communicate while I coach in this way. It helps me communicate effectively and efficiently in the chaotic environment in which I work. Thus, I taught the technique to our players.

I explained to them the premise (first I explained to them who Coach Wooden was, how he was famous for his attention to detail and focus on fundamentals (such as how at the start of every season he taught his players how to put on their socks correctly) of the +/-/+ system, why it was so powerful, and how to use it with each other. Before I knew it, there was a constant stream of "hands here, not up there, down here" and "knee out, not inside, out like this."

Leadership Education

What started out as a few players asking me for book recommendations on leadership, turned into my favorite and, in my opinion, the most unexpected physical manifestation of this entire process: the Leadership Library. This was a fantastic example of the organic development of the growing culture within our team, generated and cultivated, almost by accident, by the players themselves. I'd love to tell you I had the Leadership Library stenciled into my plans for the off-season program, but that would be a complete lie. During our one-on-one meetings, several players expressed the desire to learn more about how to lead, and since they knew I read a lot, they asked me for books on the topic. I told them that I'd be more than happy to loan them a book, on one condition. They had to take a few notes, discuss what lessons they took away with me, and then present those thoughts to the group so we could all learn something. The idea was that leadership is not defined by a title, but by actions. If you have the opportunity to help your teammates, the standard we should live by is that there is no question, you help your teammates. By presenting your thoughts on the book you've read, you've at least had to give some thought as to what the message is, and you'll be able to inform and educate everyone else at the same time. Not to mention, from a life skills standpoint, most young people can benefit from experience developing thoughts on a topic and public speaking, even if the "public" in this case are the guys they spend all their time with. What transpired from that point on was completely unexpected.

After the first two players finished their books on back to back days, and subsequently spent three or four minutes giving a brief synopsis to the team, another couple of players approached me after lift, asking if they could borrow a book. And then a few more enquired. And a few more. This continued to grow week after week, all summer long. Players were "checking out" two and three books at a time. Several players formed a book club, where they would meet every couple of days to discuss what they were learning from a particular book. We are talking about 20-year-old male college hockey  players, not exactly the expected demographic for book clubs. While I originally asked for just a brief bullet point list of the takeaways, players were voluntarily submitting full on book reports. I'm talking 14 pages written on letterhead reports.

What started out as a request by a couple of individuals especially interested in improving their leadership abilities had morphed into a semi-academic leadership and culture development weekly seminar. Over the course of our summer training we had upwards of fifteen of these reports and presentations. It was wild, and more importantly, it was helping to shape the culture that was now coming into focus. This was becoming a group highly interested in getting better and helping each other grow. They were hungry for improvement, and constantly raising the bar.

Vision

One of the most influential books I've ever read is *Start with Why* by Simon Sinek. The TED talk on the topic is exceptional and serves as a great Cliff Notes version of the book. The basic principle for anyone who hasn't read it is that the best organizations in the world look at their brand, their marketing, and their products differently than most everyone else. Most companies can tell you what they do. They can tell you how they do it. However, they generally can't tell you why they do what they do. In *Start with Why*, Sinek outlines how companies such as Apple develop their culture and their brand in reverse from the typical structure. They tell us why they exist first, explaining what their deeper purpose is. Next, they tell us how they make that vision come to life, and finally what they actually make.

> *"Everything we do, we believe in challenging the status quo. We believe in thinking differently. The way we challenge the status quo is by making our products beautifully designed, simple to use and user friendly. We just happen to make great computers. Want to buy one?"* Start With Why TED Talk

Companies that think this way are invariably loved, admired, and usually exceptionally successful, because they appeal to our basic human need to connect. Teams are no different. Without a "why," I don't believe you can have a strong culture. That "why" needs input from everyone, not just from whomever is seated at the top of the pyramid.

We talked about this concept from day one. In fact, one of the players critiques about the past year was that he didn't feel as if there was a strong, agreed upon "why." Obviously, the purpose of the team was to win games and compete for championships. But that's what everyone wants in collegiate athletics. That is the superficial reason for competing, but it wasn't anything more than that. There was nothing deeper and more meaningful behind the purpose of the team, according to most of the players. Why did they come to the rink every day? Why did they lift weights and practice? Obvious answers superficially, but deep down, why? I posed this question to all the players in the initial survey, as well as the one-on-one meetings I had with them. "Why do you play hockey?" That is really the key. Deep down, what drives you? I wanted each player to spend some genuine time hashing over this in his own mind. Many had never thought deeply about it. But almost all came back with, "love of the game," "it's what makes me happiest" or some variation on these. Some were even more prophetic: "I want my biological father to see me on tv someday and realize what he's missed." Talk about a strong "WHY."

What was the point of this? Why did this matter? Because in order to have a deep, unwavering commitment to something bigger than yourself, that something has to matter to you. It has to matter deeply. If you don't have a true "why," then when things get tough, you'll head in the other direction. Angela Duckworth talks about this in her book, *Grit*. That applies for the individual, as well as for the team. Some may call this a vision statement, and I wouldn't disagree. Whatever one wants to call it, if it isn't agreed upon and tied into everyone in the group, you are going to have weak links in the culture chain.

The team needed to decide what mattered to them…why they even cared and what would motivate them to be "gritty" in the dog days of the season, when it would be so much easier just to back off a bit. This was the longest and most challenging part of the process during the summer. In fact, it took until the team came back on campus at the start of the fall before they ultimately decided on a "why." Earlier that summer, they had come to me with the motto or catch phrase that they believed best encapsulated their reason for training…not quite a fully formed "why", but an important step, nonetheless.

Pay The Man.

These three words, borrowed from Josh Bridges, a Navy Seal and CrossFit competitor, became the easily understood, quickly recalled, and deeply held belief that carried with it the connotation of the purpose of daily struggle. Simply put, it means "Rent is due. Put in the work. Nothing great comes without sacrifice." This line became the rallying cry of our group, repeated in times of struggle, spoken in celebration of hard work, and as a reminder of the unifying vision behind the culture of our group, even as that was being developed and hashed out. As an ode to the great Greg Popovich, head coach of the San Antonio Spurs (and a favorite of one of our assistant coaches who frequently passes around articles and interviews of "Pop" in the office), we had a sign constructed for our weight room with the words "PAY THE MAN" boldly displayed, along with the phrase in each language spoken on our team. If you are at all familiar with the culture surrounding the San Antonio Spurs, you know that inclusion is hugely important for them. Making sure that players and staff, assembled from all over the world feel welcome and supported is a key component of Pop's overarching philosophy. They have their motto along with other signage around the facility in the native language of everyone on the team. Inclusion.

The History of the Program

One of the things I realized early on, while reflecting back on what we had missed as a staff, was we failed to appreciate that none of the players had, at this point, been involved with the program during our first few years. None of the current players were on our team when we inherited a program with only five wins. None of the players on our current team went through the early struggles to change a culture and create belief and accountability to a common purpose, to come out on the other side and within two years, played in the Frozen Four. We forgot that while we as a staff had been here for 8 years, our oldest players had only been here for four. In fact, the senior class from the past season was the first group that did not have a direct connection to any of the players who were involved with the development of our program from the ground up. In my opinion, this was an important missing point. We expected our team to know what we knew, to remember what we remembered, but we forgot that they literally didn't know what the past looked like. How could they, unless we taught it to them? This was the first team not to have any real insight or link into what it took to become good again. It's human nature to gloss over the struggle and recall only the end product. We had fallen into this trap, and the consequences reverberated through our program. There was tremendous struggle early on, and that continuous progression was what resulted in our accomplishments over time. However, outside of the coaching staff, no one else was actually present and connected to that process.

The current team had no idea about these struggles and from where we had come. That was our major failing. We expected the culture that had been developed and passed along to continue, and we forgot that culture is like a garden, just because it has given you tomatoes doesn't mean you don't need to keep tending to it if you want to get your cucumbers.

We had failed to teach our players what it meant to be a "Lowell Man." We certainly said those words often along with the motto that hung high on the wall in our dressing room, but none of the players really understood it. It was just something the coaches said. There was no connection. Fortunately, one of the greatest examples of a "Lowell Man" happened to still be training with me, during the summer before his then fifth pro season.

Josh Holmstrom is the epitome of what it means to be a Lowell hockey player. Tough, gritty, hardworking, blue collar…he is essentially the poster child for the city of Lowell. And he is one of the greatest captains to ever wear our sweater. I asked him if he'd be interested in speaking with the team near the end of the summer. I wanted him to give the current team a sense of what things were like before they arrived on campus. Before the new lounge and locker room. Before the performance center. Before the luxury boxes. Before a sold-out building, NHL scouts, and even matching workout gear. Josh was in the gym every day before the team, with the rest of our alumni group, so I knew the players were at least familiar with him. They knew how long he'd played professionally, mostly in the minors, and they knew the commitment and love of the game it takes to ride the busses for that long. They saw him every day, early in the morning, training, sweating, working, with his toothless grin, as if out of a bad hockey movie. He had credibility, the leadership skills, and most importantly, he cared deeply about the team and the program, and hated seeing from the outside what had happened the previous season. He was excited for the opportunity to impart some wisdom to our young and hungry team.

Josh spoke to our group and explained to them how much the team meant to all the alums, how, while riding busses from town to town in the minors they would all text each other after Lowell games, updating scores and stats, and sharing stories. How they had little when he came here…an unheralded team without the clout of some of the "bigger schools," without the bells and whistles, and early on, without the wins. That has changed; the culture had changed. Lowell had become a force in Hockey East and on the national stage. The "Men of Lowell" were reviled as opponents. Tough, hard, disciplined. Another coach had remarked that it seemed as if there were ten of them on the ice when they got rolling, and how it was nearly impossible to play against Lowell…they just kept coming. Relentless. How they were all so close…a brotherhood. They worked hard. They played hard. And they took care of each other. Josh Holmstrom expressed to our team what I never had and never could. What it meant to be a Lowell Man. The pride of being part of this great history. This resonated deeply with the team. This "Lesson in Lowell" continued into the preseason as our coaches organized a short field trip to the Lowell National Historic Park (much of the downtown in the city of Lowell is actually a National Park) where our players were taken on a guided walking tour through one of the many old textile mills that made up Lowell, and served as one of the most important early centers for the industrial revolution. This experience helped to solidify the blue collar, gritty, hardworking roots that define the

city and the identity of our team. Connecting the players to the history of the community and its place in the world was an eye opening and moving experience.

About that Why

The culmination of the culture development program was the defining "vision statement," if you will. As the players returned to campus for the start of school, just a few short weeks since the end of our summer training program, they reconvened to iron out their thoughts on a collective "WHY." They asked for my input, the coaches' thoughts and direction, and ultimately settled on their own, self-described purpose. This statement was drawn from all they had learned and all they had taught each other. From the early stages of the off-season, they learned, recited, and then took hold of much of the verbal aspects of coaching each other. They were willing to learn to hold themselves and each other accountable, and to "Pay The Man" when the rent was due. From the experiences of struggling together, overcoming obstacles, and enjoying the process, they found their "WHY."

Culture is the foundation to which everything else within an organization will be built upon. The size and strength of that culture will ultimately influence the heights to which a team may grow. If the culture of a group is strong, the other great aspects of the development and performance program will be able to flourish. Training, sport science, nutrition, leadership: if it matters, there will be a place for it at the table when a strong culture is in place. However, if the culture is allowed to wither, the scapegoats will be these same areas of influence when the inevitable decline in success creeps in. It is culture, or "the way we do things around here," that matters most.

This journey in search of culture development has been both strategic and organic. It has been an undertaking which has been as much driven from the bottom up, as from the top down. And it is an ever-ongoing process. After all, if culture can slip because of a lack of dedicated focus, doesn't it make sense that growth needs to be continuously managed? Throughout this process, I have gained a greater appreciation for the behind-the-scenes work it takes to keep a ship moving in the right direction. Though there is no one-size-fits-all approach to improving organizational culture, hopefully I've been able to outline a template that might fit for you, in whatever situation and role you may find yourself. If nothing else, I can say the process has been fun, and I'm looking forward to where our team goes next.

REFERENCES

Kerr, J. M. (2013). *Legacy*. London: Constable.

Turner, A. N., Bishop, C., Cree, J., Carr, P., Mccann, A., Bartholomew, B., & Halsted, L. (2018). Building A High-Performance Model for Sport. *Strength and Conditioning Journal, 1*. doi:10.1519/ssc.0000000000000447

Kraus, M. W., Huang, C., & Keltner, D. (2010). Tactile Communication, Cooperation, and Performance: An Ethological Study of the NBA. *Emotion, 10*(5), 745-749.

Coyle, D. (2019). *Culture Code: The secrets of highly successful groups*. New York: Random House.

Walter, E. (2013, October 01). 50 Heavyweight Leadership Quotes. Retrieved from https://www.forbes.com/sites/ekaterinawalter/2013/09/30/50-heavyweight-leadership-quotes/#3082d5b82259

Sinek, S. (2013). *Start with Why: How Great Leaders Inspire Everyone to Take Action*. London: Portfolio/Penguin.

Wooden, J., & Carty, J. (2015). *Coach Wooden's Pyramid of Success*. Grand Rapids, MI: Revell, a division of Baker Publishing Group.

Coyle, D. (2009). *The talent code: Greatness Isn't Born. It's Grown. Here's How*. New York: Bantam Books.

Michael Boyle's Strengthcoach.com Blog. (n.d.). Retrieved from https://strengthcoachblog.com/tag/john-wooden/

Sinek, S. (n.d.). How Great Leaders Inspire Action. Retrieved from https://www.ted.com/talks/simon_sinek_how_great_leaders_inspire_action?language=en

Who is Devan McConnell?

Devan McConnell was named the Head Hockey Performance Coach at UMASS Lowell in 2014.

In this role, he is responsible for the oversight and development of all aspects of physical development for the Ice Hockey team, including strength, speed, and power development, energy system development, nutrition, recovery and regeneration, physiological monitoring, sport science, technology integration, as well as coordination of analytics, long term athletic development, and tactical periodization. In addition to this role, he is responsible for the physical development of the Field Hockey team.

McConnell was named UMass Lowell's first Director of Sports Performance in September of 2011. The position was tasked with integrating a cutting-edge sports performance program into the University's athletic department. At the time, UMass Lowell had never had a dedicated Performance Director or Sports Performance program. Under his direction, a comprehensive performance-based model was introduced, focusing on movement quality, athletic development, and injury reduction strategies.

Devan is regularly invited to speak on topics of sport science, performance development, and recovery and regeneration. In addition, he co-authored a book on the holistic implementation of sport science called "INTENT: A Practical Approach to Applied Sport Science for Athletic Development".

Prior to joining UMass Lowell, McConnell served as the Sports Performance Coordinator at Stanford University from 2008-11. He worked closely with the women's basketball team, along with men's and women's volleyball, all of which were regulars in the NCAA Tournament. During his tenure, Women's basketball competed in 3 straight Final Fours, the Women's volleyball team competed in two Final Fours, the men's volleyball program won the 2010 NCAA Championship.

While at Stanford, McConnell also served as the Performance Education Coordinator, instructing the Cardinals' personnel, building a staff library and scheduling guest speakers. He continues in his role as educator, both as an Adjunct Professor within the Department of Physical Therapy at Lowell, and as an internationally recognized speaker on all topics of performance enhancement. Devan has also authored multiple articles on strength and conditioning for ice hockey.

Before his appointment to Stanford, McConnell worked at Mike Boyle Strength and Conditioning, one of the leading sports performance facilities in the Northeast. He also spent time working with three NHL teams, the Anaheim Ducks, San Jose Sharks, and Boston Bruins.

McConnell is a certified Performance Enhancement Specialist and Corrective Exercise Specialist through the National Academy of Sports Medicine (NASM). He is also a Functional Movement Screen Specialist. In addition, he is a nationally and internationally recognized speaker on the topics of hockey, physiological monitoring and athlete development and is regarded as one of the foremost experts in the hockey performance field.

McConnell received his Bachelor's degree in Exercise Science from Fitchburg State in 2008. While attending Fitchburg State, he was a standout hockey player, twice recognized as the team's Most Valuable Player and was in contention for All America honors. He also holds a Master's degree in Exercise Science, Performance Enhancement and Injury Prevention from California University.

A native of Lake Stevens, Washington, McConnell resides in Groton, Massachusetts with his wife Erica, and their two children, Finnegan and Dublin.

7

The Team Behind the Team

The Real Meaning of a Successful "Multi-Integrative" Approach

Keenan Robinson

Sports Medicine and Science Director

USA Swimming

A "Sport Performance Team" or "High Performance Director" have become hot topic titles and terms in the sporting world, as common as GPS, performance nutrition, ACWL (acute to chronic workload), culture, and the process. All are great entities to apply to your athletes and organizations, when intent is defined clearly, and the correct people are managing the entities. Non-siloed or integrated teams is the start but is often said more to make a positive impression than on actual in-the-trenches implementation. Allow us the opportunity to look at some potential topics to consider when creating the "team behind the team."

The director or manager is often a term given by human resources to differentiate job duties and often pay scale. However, I would propose in sports that leadership starts with the Head Coach and the team physician. I understand, this is a book for strength coaches, this author serves as one. I don't want to devalue the importance in our leadership, but when all factors are considered, should Johnny All American gets hurt or Susy Gold Medalist gets sick, the coach determines their replacement and the doctor sets the parameters for rehab or return to participation. Strength coaches don't get to contribute in the selection of the coaches for whom we work. However, in the world of revenue sports the coach often selects us, so it seems beyond the scope of this book to go into a sport coach or SPP coach contribution to our support staff. So, first consider the physician and his team and evaluate our approach when thinking about how to communicate with them.

The Physician

Regardless of a college or professional setting, the team physician ultimately signs the athlete's physical exam for full participation, modified participation, or disqualification. So as a strength coach, trying to undercut a physician decision or go beyond the scope of your practice and diagnose will not be an athlete-first approach and more than likely have you end up in a GM/AD's office or court room. I appreciate and understand that they don't necessarily understand a Prilepin Chart as well as us, but it should be remembered that they did attend medical school and as such focused their attention on the human body and how it operates. Therefore, they most likely understand energy system development, CNS response to training, and musculotendinous biologics better than might generally be realized.

Much like a baseball team has the "skipper", in addition to various assistant coaches, , a bullpen manager, a roving fielding instructor, a hitting instructor, and a other specialty coaches, the head team physician has his other team of family practice internal medicine, sports fellow trained, neurologist, cardiologist, allergist/pulmonologist and subsidiaries of orthopedics(shoulder, hip, ankle, knee, back) to whom they refer out to when warranted. Collectively, their primary goal is to make sure an athlete has the requisite health to participate in the sport. They enjoy the thrill of victory and are usually extremely supportive, but safety is never compromised.

As you and your strength staff analyze a season that just ended as well as the upcoming season, some commonalities usually arise: injury rate(both players lost for the season and those that were managed throughout the season but were rarely operating above 80%), fatigue during games/competitions(wearing down in the 4th quarter) and at the end of the season(played exhausted in March/April or we worn out by the time post season began), or subjective lack of one or multiple biological/ metabolic properties(we looked weak and got pushed around or they simply had nothing left to give at the end of all their races). Perhaps you followed Joel Jamison's ESD plan to a tee, but somehow the performance and even your tracking didn't connect. As you ponder what went wrong it could have been a factor as simple as your indoor training facility causing an increase in allergic responses in your athletes. A PFT(pulmonary function test) might reveal that not only were your athletes fighting an infection for the season, but they may have been on the wrong medication from the start of treatment (albuterol will not fix all respiratory issues).

Perhaps you are looking at the season ahead and working on your periodization (although you may not agree with the concept of periodization, I would ask you to consider the work of Vladimir Issurin, Tudor Bompa as well as contemporary contributors to this topic including Dr. Chris Morris or Louie Simmons) At this point you want to implement ways to develop power, max strength, hypertrophy, alactic proficiency, top end speed repeatability, or aerobic capacity. You believe you have taken into consideration all variables: off-season training sessions permitted by NCAA, CBA off-season practice sessions, spring training duration, and the season itself. Take some time to review these phases with your physician team, emphasizing these points: 1) it will make them aware of expectations for the athletes throughout the season, 2) it will allow for productive discussion on programming manipulation, and 3) for those athletes coming off seasons in which they were hurt/ ill, it allows for properly tailoring for them to return robust and greater ability to withstand the rigors of the approaching season. Remember the greatest predictor of injury is the history of a previous injury. So, if you may have a defensive end returning from back injuries who wasn't doing a great deal of lower extremity activity. If you don't consider the tendon loading properties described by Jill Cook and her colleagues you may have too much oversight into their COD activities and that lineman could reinjure his Achilles. While it's not necessary to be an authority on Dr. Cooks writings (although exposure to her work is a worthwhile investment), your orthopedic surgeon will have priceless insight into a logical progression when the athlete resumes jumps, sprint work, and high velocity varied agility work. Finally, when you are in season and so many of your starters are in a "modified state" except on game day, be aware of the potential interactions with medications athletes are prescribed. Perhaps your athlete is placed on a floraquinallin. It would be a serious matter to not have familiarity with that medication. Furthermore, side effects of the medication must be considered if you maintain your in-season medicine ball strength speed programming not realizing the pharmacological side effect is tendon disruption and a shooting guard could rupture his pec minor tendon. These examples of potential actual sports season situations should keenly emphasize the need for incorporation of your team physician into your weekly one-on-one meetings, just as you do with the head coach and his assistants. It might serve well to extend the "proverbial olive branch" and invite them to training sessions to observe how the coaching, exercise selection, and loading parameters utilized by you and your staff. I've heard of a number of occasions in which a strength coach observed a surgical procedure and shared how revealing the experience was. So, consider reciprocating that favor with the physicians.

The Athletic Trainer

The biggest turf war in athletics could be "the trainer v the trainer" although neither of those professions prefer that term. At any rate, some facts should be noted: the athletic trainer communicates with the head coach(as do you); the athletic trainer communicates with the team physician(as I've encouraged you to do in the previous section), the athletic trainer communicates with the AD/GM(who often is the only third party auditor in sports); and finally, yet most importantly, the athletic trainer is in constant daily interaction with the athletes. I wish to stress the importance of these relationships. If athletes sense a rift in their support team, doubt would well arise and eventually starts to cause athletes to "pick sides" which is not conductive to positive results. Even though, I am a certified athletic trainer don't exonerate our field. I wish more of my ATC peers that have sat for and passed the NSCA's CSCS examination would apply that by training themselves. More importantly, using that knowledge to integrate with the strength staffs programming and implementation. Communication is so much easier when the language/ terminology is the same. Let's start with some elementary commonalities that may aid in bridging a potential divide between the two groups:

1. Pre-Season Physical Exam- This seem to be a perfect opportunity for both parties to review all of their "rule in/ rule out" assessments, motor control evaluations, movement competencies, and risk factor assessments. A model demonstrated this at the top level was at Stanford University with Scott Anderson (ATC) and Shannon Turley (S&C). Even when the man with khaki pants departed, Stanford continued to field healthy, quick, resilient, and championship teams. So, whether both parties agree on FMS or their own standard assessment protocol, both staffs are present to help the athletes win. Finally, as discussed earlier, this is an occasion for a team physician to be present. So, without much effort we have found the unicorn, so to speak, an integrated model.

2. The daily or game day "Preparatory Session"- while not desiring to discuss at this juncture the implementation of "activation" or "dynamic warm up", I recommend the systems of Charlie Weingroff or Tim Pelot from a strength

coaches perspective or any of the pitching coaches from the AZ Diamondbacks or Bob Bowman from a sport coach perspective(because anytime Randy Johnson took the mound or Michael Phelps stood on the block, they brought their A game). Of major significance is how this can become a more effective initiative. Let's propose that we are implementing this for injury prevention purposes. So then, let's address it in movements akin to the epidemiology paradigm.

- Engage in a conversation with the sport coaches/position coaches to identify what they will be having their athletes perform from the time their athletes/ teams arrive at a venue for a competition until to the start of the game or individual event. It would be worthwhile to have the same information on training days. Once you as a strength coach have that information you can evaluate your checklist of goals of an activation session, determine what won't be achieved by the sport coach, and then program a session for the missing elements.

- With your ongoing conversations with sports medicine, you'll already be equipped with information regarding joint ranges of motion that these athletes possess, individual modifications for those returning from or managing injuries Then you will be able to take what you already know of the required movement ranges needed for the sport activity and create truly beneficial movement works

- Finally incorporate the sports science element of force plate testing, readiness management, or physiology monitoring to ensure a truly advantageous preparatory session.

3. On a day-to-day weight room/ conditioning session, truly groundbreaking initiatives can occur. It is here that both sports medicine and strength can put great care on an athlete's well-being. Instead of having a prehab session, weight session (in which other prehab activities are usually incorporated), injury treatment model, all of this can be accomplished by having both

practitioners involved with writing and implementing the daily/ weekly/ monthly sessions. I encourage this thought process for the following reasons:

- The goal of both rehab/prehab and strength training is applying stress for a specific adaptation to occur. So, exercise selection, sets/reps, intensity, and tempo are used by both professions. Thus, having just have one all-encompassing session is not an optimal use of time. Athletes don't work out: they train. Healthy athletes don't do physical therapy, they train their deficiencies to bring them up to "normal" levels. Once this concept is understood the daily sessions suddenly become truly impactful for the athlete, and there is more compliance in all domains.

- Both in-season or for the year-round training sports injury (or modified training) will occur. Therefore, identify what needs to be modified and why. Is it movement or loading restriction? Then both the ATC and strength coach can review their data base of modifications, which are actually exercise preferences, in order to return to the originally activity. Loading reduction happens even in the healthy population (Louie Simmons has written well and extensively on the topic of Westside Periodization). I introduce this to athletes as an opportunity for supercompensation to occur as opposed to a reduction.

The Chiropractor

The addition or incorporation of an American Chiropractic Board of Sports Physicians certified Sports Physician and Diplomate can be invaluable. These doctors have gone through a strenuous academic curriculum specific to sports pathologies and management of athletes. Beyond their ability to quickly and efficiently treat an athlete with an osteopathic injury, often times (and improperly) called a crack or pop, sports chiropractors often have a CSCS accreditation as well, so they understand and speak the strength coach's language. In addition, their years of clinical experience seeing common injuries and dysfunctions, especially with sporting populations can lead to helping you program exercises with less "risk factor" or add your creation of exercise alternative data base.

First, their clinical assessment and approach to movement may include aspects that you and your staff can add to its need's analysis (or movement screen) as I've discussed in the other HP team member sections. Instead of a general quadruped internally rotated/ adducted shoulder, whilst performing torso rotation as your assessment of thoracic spine kinematics, a sports chiropractor can help you understand the three-dimensional movement properties of the spine and why so often treat the T3- T8 area. This can reinforce why mere foam roll extension activities or side lying upper body clams aren't enough for modalities to keep this area healthy. Sports chiropractors are so often asked to treat the sacroiliac area after low back pain occurs. They possess an expert understanding of those three innominate bones and the way in which mechanics or poor movement quality happens in athletes can impact that area of the back. In addition, and perhaps more importantly they can recommend interventions to incorporated beforehand or exercises to program so that the most comprehensive and effective program can be provided for your athletes.

Second, one skill set often overlooked in a sports chiropractor is their soft tissue skill set. Many of these practitioners have certification in commercial fascia treatment models, so they are very keen in adaptive shortening as well as tendon/ ligament pathologies. A collaboration with DC can help initially in your pre/ post training foam roller and trigger point sessions. Although extremely effective and having their purpose in the strength program, a discussion and plan in conjunction with sports DC's can make these sessions more beneficial. For example, the foam rolling session may revolve more around common soft tissue dysfunctions seen in that specific sport populations (i.e. groin/ adductors in soccer or patella/ quad tendon in basketball). Additionally, the chronic injury athlete/athlete populations may get a more beneficial routine from you and your staff if that athlete understands that by using trigger point products to address specific muscle/muscle groups prior to certain lifts, this will: a) make the lift more efficient and will yeild the full benefits and b) prevent the unnecessary cycle/ discussion of "exercise A causes this type of injury" and instead change the narrative of putting the athlete into an environment to succeed on particular lifts. When you combine both aspects, your program is enhanced immediately because you have intentional and purposeful warmups and an injury prevention aspect.

The Sport Physiologist/ Sports Scientist

The sport physiologist could be a valuable asset for optimizing current performance potential of the athletes in your care or for teams your supporting. First, a physiologist must have received a masters or PhD in the study of human biology and physiology. So, by that educational route, they have extensively studied stress adaptation, environmental considerations, and periodization and peaking considerations.

When incorporating the services and skill sets of a physiologist, I start by tasking them with tasking them with readily attainable initiatives. Consider the tests you plan to perform in preseason, in season, and post season to evaluate the efficacy of your program. Then task the physiologist with auditing your thought process by having them list the biological properties they can measure to objectively answer the testing questions so as to better individualize your programming. Typically, in land sports, strength & conditioning coaches perform some form of preseason energy system/conditioning test that either: a) evaluates the fitness level of the team upon returning to organized team activities or sets the plan for in season cardiovascular activities. The physiologist should be asked to first start with an evaluation the exact demands of the sporting activity on the cardiopulmonary system and, if necessary, break down positional or individual needs. Next, have them critically appraise your previous programming and see where there are ways to: 1) enable greater syncing up with the actual demands of the sport, 2) identify gaps in your programming at fully developing an aerobic system or truly expressing speed qualities, 3) allow for optimal stress exposure and recuperation time. The outcome is a conditioning program based on sound science with practical implementation.

Environmental considerations for both training and competition are often an afterthought in sports. Environmental impacts are not limited exclusively to heat and humidity, precipitation, and frigid temperatures, but often all of those factors combined must be measured. As I mentioned previously, your physiologist has extensive educational background in human physiology. Therefore, something as simple as getting a legitimate evaluation of each team member's pulmonary system in response to the training facility you use is important. Asthma medications are often administered haphazardly, without full evaluation of potential allergic reaction to the air quality in your training location. A simple preseason testing day could potentially uncover athletes operating at sub-optimal lung capacity. Another environmental consideration that has been absolutely bastardized in sports performance is altitude training. Instead of squandering budget funds on those masks, I encourage every reader to instead purchase "High Altitude Training for Sports" by Dr. Randy Wilber in order to more appropriately apply altitude training. Dr. Wilber's resume as a sport performance authority vested in high altitude training is without equal as evidenced by the Olympic success of athletes whom he has guided.

A final recommendation of using a sports physiologist is that of the "hot toy" sleep monitoring. The tool you choose to monitor sleep quality should be based on polysomnography. Become familiar with this basic sleep science before you commence monitoring, and then use a cheap but effective tool, such as a questionnaire. This will allow you as the strength coach to determine whether it's a sleep hygiene or sleep quality/quantity issue impacting your athletes. If the team is complaint with this impactful, yet inexpensive model, then incorporate validated monitoring devices. The physiologist can be tremendously impactful at overlaying the strength & conditioning program with athletes sleep responses. To truly see the impact a physiologist can have on "High Performance," consider what Nic Gill's impact on the New Zealand All Blacks rugby program.

To end with a cliché of "integrated team approach" or operating without silos can be a disservice to this manual and you the reader. I encourage you as a high-level coach to go back a review at the sections that were highlighted or notes written on the side of the page to: first, how have I sold my program short by not considering some of the writings; second, look at service providers you have in place and review the recommendations to determine potential; thirdly, your plan for the future should take into account staff changes or your financial resources to expand. Instead of purchasing GPS, sleep monitors, or extraneous weight room toys, bring on a staff member who will fill a void on your "performance roster." Through being practical you heighten the degree of daily impactful performance in the disciplined pursuit of excellence.

Who is Keenan Robinson?

Keenan Robinson joined USA Swimming as the Sports Medicine & Science Director in 2016.

Keenan is responsible for evaluating injury epidemiology in National Team swimmers, identifying risk factors, and streamlining medical care for Team USA swimmers to reduce training time loss or surgical procedures.

An NATABOC certified athletic trainer and NSCA certified strength and conditioning coach, Keenan brings 15 years of direct swimming support at the club (North Baltimore Aquatic Club), university (Michigan and Arizona State), and international level. He has served on Olympic and World Championship medical staffs, bringing a unique skill set to the sport through both performance and medicine.

Keenan is believed to be the only strength coach, from a strength and conditioning perspective, to have programmed and coached three different swimmers to World Championship titles while they were in high school, college, and then post-graduate careers. He has provided day-to-day performance medicine care for teams across the USA Swimming membership spectrum that have won Sectional, Junior National, NCAA, and National titles. Keenan also serves on the 8-member USOC Sports Medicine Standards Advisory Group.

Keenan's extensive experience in evaluating and implementing physiological and biological measures have led to performance improvements in swimming. As a sought-after keynote speaker, he has presented at NATA, ACSM, NSCA, ACBSP, and the AMSSM national conference.

He has been published in the Journal of Athletic Training, Current Sports Medicine Reports, and is in the process of co-authoring of two textbooks. He enjoys training for power lifting, cooking, and all Detroit sports.

He resides in Colorado Springs with his wife Kalyn, a Defense Intelligence Agency analyst and 2004 Olympic swimmer, and their two children Regan Molly and Roch Ignatius.

8

Boring Stuff That Works

Andrew Althoff

Assistant AD for Sports Performance

Baylor University

There is a lot of boring stuff that works within performance. The following pages are designed to give the reader heuristics which have been learned over the years by reading, paying attention to the seemingly mundane, and taking notes. This should not be interpreted as a lack of belief in high level monitoring, fancy supersets, or complex complexes. However, ensuring 90% of the program is kept simple will typically ease the execution. If the simple cannot be executed, we do not deserve anything fancy. Additionally, if the training is bad, we are monitoring bad training. Occam's razor is generally used to describe a mindset where processes should not increase beyond what is necessary. Hopefully, this razor-like explanation of a holistic approach to performance provides enough detail to give clarity without bogging down the reader with unnecessary thoughts, opinions or information. Before climbing up the pyramid, we must first start with the base of coaching philosophy.

Layer 1 – Philosophical Simplicity

Every sport has its complexities. These intricacies can be addressed by ensuring a simple, yet all-encompassing philosophy to ensure the athletes not only succeed during competition but socially inside and outside the organization. Therefore, all decisions will be made by keeping the best interest of the athletes in mind for both their short and long-term success. As we reflect further into programming for our athletes, we can consider things such as genetics, body types, mental ability, stamina, requirements of the sport, schematic demands, facility availability, in addition to social and environmental factors. Taking all this into consideration can be overwhelming and prevent us from making tangible progress. Therefore, we will focus on three main performance areas: injury prevention, performance enhancement and mental development.

Regardless of what cutting edge technology or groundbreaking technique is out there, the primary goal of any performance team should be injury prevention. We know injuries generally happen for three reasons: 1) the athlete was not adequately prepared for the stress which occurred (controllable), 2) something unexpected happened for which the athlete could not have been prepared (uncontrollable), or 3) an imbalance between nature and nurture (things we may be predisposed to base on anthropometrics, mental health, or injury history but can be minimized if accommodations are made). We also know healthy muscles and joints decrease the chance of injury. Additionally, when an injury occurs in a properly conditioned and well-trained athlete, they will typically heal faster and spend less time in limited participation.

Based on this information, we know there is a symbiotic relationship between injury prevention and performance enhancement. Performance enhancement is achieved by emphasizing strength, speed, power, agility, flexibility, body composition, nutrition and conditioning. By addressing these areas with a collaborative approach, we can better help athletes meet the demand of their sport – not the latest fad.

For mental development, athletes must be trained to maintain a high level of focus, maturity, accountability, disciplined competitiveness, and loyalty. Additionally, we want to teach our athletes to manage their distractions, improving their level of focus, giving them the confidence needed to prepare and compete at the highest level. Within a large organization it will be difficult to monitor all athletes at all times. Therefore, we must provide resources and education to our athletes before giving them the autonomy to be the CEO of their own company. Additionally, it will be of utmost importance to identify those within the organization who are critical to the team's success and ensure they remain at the forefront of services provided. Heraclitus, a famous Greek philosopher, is quoted as saying, "Out of every hundred men, ten should not even be there, eighty are just targets, nine are the real fighters, and we are lucky to have them, for they make the battle. Ah, but the one, one is a warrior, and he will bring the others back." While every person inside the organization is important, each individual will have a different level of successful contribution depending on their current skillset and career. Misidentifying the key contributors for a given season within the organization (this may not only be limited to the athletic population) will be costly. By ensuring we flood those contributors with services to help keep them available for the entirety of the season, we can keep the ship afloat until it is the next generation's turn to take over.

It is not only the decisions athletes make at the facility which will have an effect on their success, but those away from the facility as well. These choices will mutually drive their personal development as well as the growth of the organization. In summary, the person you are determines the athlete you will be. In an age of quick remedies, social media promises and provides 24-hour access, this message cannot be emphasized enough.

Layer 2 – Assessing Progress and Measuring Success

Implementation of any performance program should revolve around the mantra, "do no harm." By answering the three basic questions of what, why, and how, we can improve the athlete's physiological qualities, enhance their mental development and dig into the three areas of injury prevention. After answering these questions, we can then develop a concise plan for further application. Through motivating our athletes to do work with intent by attacking these categories during the training session, it would provide the basis for the accumulation of marginal gains. The stacking of success over time would put us in a position to win and give us something to focus our eyes on other than the competition.

1. Prevent Injuries

- Question (Q): What?
  - Answer (A): Although some injuries are unforeseen, there are steps which can be taken during training to limit such occurrences.
- Q: Why?
  - A: Athletes must be consistently available for competition.
- Q: How?
  - A: Healthy muscles and joints decrease the risk of injury. Additionally, a well-trained and nutritionally disciplined athlete will typically recover faster from an injury.

The Plan

- Collaborate with other departments such as sports medicine, sports science and nutrition to utilize objective and subjective assessments/monitoring techniques and tools to gauge the status of the athlete's wellness and performance.
- A simplistic training regime, which will be individualized as needed, will ensure athletes are executing exercises and drills to activate all muscles and joints using appropriate ranges of motion.
- Assist the nutrition staff with counseling and education to limit the amount of muscle pulls, cramps, and other nutrition-related injury concerns.

2. Improve Physiological Qualities

- Q: What?
  - A: Improve physiological abilities as they relate to peak sport performance and injury prevention: strength, power, speed, agility, flexibility, mobility, body composition, and conditioning.
- Q: Why?
  - A: Many qualities affect the overall physical performance of the athletes.
- Q: How?
  - A: Train the qualities which will directly improve ability as it relates to the specific sport.

The Plan

- Specificity in training as applicable.
- Prioritize multi-joint movements to emphasize hip and core strength.
- Increase athleticism with complimentary exercise movements.
- Choose athleticism-enhancing drills which favor movement in space.
- Use objective and subjective assessments to monitor athlete wellness and performance.
- Through collaboration, identify the shifting physiological demands throughout the year with other departments to help coordinate the optimization of regeneration, recovery, and each athlete's unique body composition.

3. Enhance Mental Development

- **Q: What?**
  - **A:** Provide an inclusive environment for unique training scenarios to develop: focus, maturity, accountability, responsibility, discipline, competitiveness.
- **Q: Why?**
  - A: By fostering a demanding, committed and caring environment, we can make a positive impact on the mind, body and soul of each athlete.
- **Q: How?**

- **A:** Enhance all mental aspects as they relate to peak sport performance, team cohesiveness, mental toughness, emotional stability, and social responsibility.

The Plan

- Enthusiasm is mandatory.
- Have a creative yet disciplined approach to training to foster teamwork, mental toughness, and increased confidence in one's self and teammates.
- Demand proper execution of all drills, exercises, policies and procedures as they pertain to the safety and success of the organization.

If everything is important, then nothing is important. By condensing performance into these three categories we are providing specific areas to address. However, they are still general enough to give other coaches, support staff, and administrators autonomy within their respective areas of expertise and responsibility.

Layer 3 – Performance Development

Athletes must be able to display strength, power, and speed to excel at their sport, as well as the work capacity (general conditioning) to be able to do it repeatedly throughout practices and games for the length of the season. It is important to note all qualities are trained simultaneously with varying degrees of emphasis depending on the level. For example, if we are focusing on strength development, it is still important to keep a moderate amount of volume in for work capacity and power with a small amount of speed work. As we progress up to power, we would then transition to a moderate focus on speed and strength while maintaining a small amount of work capacity. Additionally, the following information is heuristic in nature and will require collaboration among all departments with the use of technology, as well as the coaches' eyes to continually evaluate and progress the athlete correctly. It is important to base these progressions by considering the training age and not birth date or at which level they are currently playing.

For the purpose of giving specifics, the following qualities outlined will help give categories for athletic development. However, it is critical to remember everything is connected. Our main responsibility will be to assess limiting factors in an individual's performance and remove them through collaboration with other departments throughout the organization. This can be done by creating a learning assessment which will give us numbers to help identify key performance indicators for identifying and evaluating talent. We must be constantly asking ourselves the questions:

- What general qualities do all athletes need?

- What are the peak forces needed? If they are too low can the athlete get hurt?

- What general qualities does this specific position (ex: pitcher, offensive lineman, sprinter, etc.) need?

- How does this vary within the specific position (ex: offensive lineman – center vs. right tackle)?

- What is their starting point/where are they now?

- Where can we get them?

- Where do they need to go?

As each respective department provides input into the evaluation process, a battery of evaluations should be run to help answer these questions and, over time, create a physical assessment to help standardize the testing conducted and evaluation protocols. For example, strength and conditioning coaches can use variations of exercises such as double/single leg squats, hinges, push-ups, pull-ups, static/dynamic holds, and carries. Sports medicine can use orthopedic and cardiac assessments. Sports science can analyze GPS and muscle/force outputs, and nutrition can use body composition and survey data. By ensuring clear and transparent communication among all departments, we can collectively drive toward a universal workflow for the greater good of the organization and the individual athletes. These assessments will hinge on what is currently being done, as well as what is currently available with the end goal of creating a common assessment language. Once this is created, the athletic population can be filtered into different buckets of needs.

Layer 4 – Defining The Buckets

When it comes to physical performance, it is easiest to view a progression of four different needs which progress up a hierarchy: work capacity → strength → power → speed. Athletes will be placed into the lowest bucket of quality until the qualities derived are sufficient enough to progress to the next. (The following information has been adapted from the work of Al Vermeil, Al Miller, Johnny Parker and Rob Panariello.)

The foundational quality needed for any athlete is work capacity or general physical preparedness. At its simplest, this is "the ability to replicate work." We must remember every part of training is some form of conditioning, including lifting weights. As stress is prescribed, we want the body to respond to it appropriately. In this level, the stress we apply is for general adaptations and is used to establish baselines for endurance, strength, power and speed while fixing any factors which may limit performance as training progresses. Additional factors to be considered in this level are ones limiting the athlete's long-term development such as body composition, range of motion, force outputs or previous injury history.

Work Capacity Recommendations			
<u>Drill</u>	<u>Description</u>	<u>Sets/Reps/Intensity</u>	<u>Weekly Totals</u>
Medicine ball, Plate or Bodyweight circuits	Continuous motion at medium speed. Example exercises: Giant Circles, Woodchoppers, Front Squat, Seated ab twists, Lunge variations, Overhead press, Chest press, etc. – be creative!	2-3 sets 10-20 reps per exercise 2-3 days/week 8-16 lbs on medicine ball and plate work	500-1000 reps
Complex	Clean pull+Muscle clean+Front squat to Military press+RDL+Bent over row ***Athlete performs all movements and reps before setting down	2-3 sets 4-6 reps 2-3 days/week Large athletes 20-30% of bodyweight Intermediates 25-35% of bodyweight Small 30-40% of bodyweight	The weight may seem light but a simple calculation of tonnage reveals one set x6 each with 100 pounds on the bar will result in 3,600 pounds moved
Long Tempo Runs	Bigs x70yds, Intermediates x85yds, Skill x100yds	2-3 sets of 3-4 reps. 18 seconds to finish rep, 30 second rest between reps, 1.5 minute rest between sets	1000-1500 yds for Bigs (500yds max for 1 session)
Short Tempo Runs	Bigs x40yds, Intermediates x45yds, Skill x50yds	2-3 sets of 4-6 reps. 10 seconds to finish rep, 10 seconds rest between reps, 1.5 minutes rest between sets	1250-1750 yds for Intermediates 1000-1500 (600 yds max for 1 session)
Walk/Run #1	Athlete runs 100 yards, walks 25 yards out and back, then runs length of field again.	2-4 trips	1500-2000 yds for Skill (750 yds max for 1 session) ***Mix and match tempo, walk/run and sled prowler throughout the week to achieve yardage goals***
Walk/Run Tempo #2	Athlete runs length of field, walks width of field	2-4 laps	
Prowler/Sled March	Big steps with good knee drive performed at walking pace.	1 set of 2-3 reps for 30-50 yards. 90 lbs max total load per implement	

Assuming proper emphasis was placed on work capacity early in an athlete's off-season, the strength block is where athletes will make significant gains. For many athletes, strength is a limiting factor for performance and/or availability. For example, increases in lower body strength can improve ability in short sprints (less than 20 yards). Additionally, strength work has shown to help increase tendon strength, which helps ensure force is put into the ground and not dissipated into the joints during change of direction, thus reducing the risk of injury. One must use caution in this category as it is easy to put too much emphasis here since it is easy to measure. Additionally, too much work done here may result in a decrement in speed/power number potential.

\multicolumn{4}{c}{**Strength Recommendations**}			
<u>Drill</u>	<u>Sets/Reps</u>	<u>Intensity</u>	<u>Weekly Totals (80-150 reps between 3 categories)</u>
Squat and its variations + Deadlift	3-5 sets of 3-6 reps	70-85%	45% of weight room strength lifts
Pushes/Presses	3-5 sets of 3-6 reps	70-85%	25% of weight room strength lifts
Lower pulls (RDL, Goodmorning, Glute-ham raise)	3-5 sets of 4-8 reps (Ratio of 3:1-2 to squat i.e. for every 3 squats, the athlete should do 1-2 lower pulls)	Dependent upon exercise	35% of weight room strength lifts
Upper pulls (Chin up, Pull Up, Bent over row, etc.)	3-5 sets of 4-8 reps (Ratio of 1:1 for press i.e. for every press the athlete should do at least 1 upper pull)	Dependent upon exercise	

Force is anything capable of changing an object's state of motion. Power is the rate at which this energy is transferred or mathematically it is force multiplied by velocity (P=F*V). Therefore, by definition, we can improve power by doing two things: increasing the amount of force without having a significant deficit of velocity (strength-speed) or we can increase the velocity without having a significant deficit of force (speed-strength). An often-overlooked aspect of power is how it will help the athlete throughout the length of the season. When two players put force into the ground, the more powerful athlete with a sturdier musculoskeletal system will deliver a more forceful blow to the ground allowing them to jump higher and/or run faster. By ensuring the athletes remain dynamic throughout the competitive season we can help ensure they continue this into the post-season. Conversely, the athlete with decrements in these qualities will have increased difficulty producing on the field and staying healthy. Similar to the strength quality, we must be strategic in this area as we can create too much stiffness in the body.

Strength-Speed Recommendations			
Drill	Sets/Reps	Intensity	Weekly Totals
Clean, Snatch, Jerk	3-5 sets of 1-5 reps	60-70% of 1RM	40-80 reps
Clean Pull, Snatch Pull	3-5 sets of 1-5 reps	10% higher than what is done on clean or snatch	
Dynamic Effort Squat, Bench	3-6 sets of 2-3 reps	Less than 50-60% of 1RM	

Speed-Strength Recommendations			
Drill	Sets/Reps	Intensity	Weekly Totals
Medicine ball throws for height or distance	2-3 sets of 5-10 reps	Max effort with landing in good posture	200-400 reps
Higher rep/Lower intensity jumps (jump rope, line hops, etc.)	2-4 sets of 20-50	Low intensity with minimal contact time	
Lower rep/Higher intensity jumps (Vertical jumps, Broad jumps, Box jumps, etc.)	2-3 sets of 2-4 reps	Max effort with landing in good posture	
Resisted sprints	2-4 reps of 10-20 yards	Resistance should not lower speed by more than 10% of the max effort	
Work in this category should be done at low intensity and a preparatory level early in training periods			

Speed is the level to which all the earlier qualities build up and, therefore, requires a sound progression to help ensure this stressor can be applied with relative safety and minimal injury risk. Due to the extreme mechanical and energetic demands of speed training, full recovery should be provided between work bouts (a simple rule, although not always achievable, is 1 minute of rest for every 10 yards sprinted). We must be strategic with the volume applied in this category as it can be the riskiest from a training standpoint, however, it can also have the biggest reward. Additionally, athletes who exhibit high amounts of speed can also be at the greatest risk of injury. The nature of this work will require the athlete to be sound in areas outside of training such as nutrition, sleep and others to help minimize this concern.

Speed Recommendations			
Quality	Description	Example	Weekly Totals
Acceleration	Rate of change	5-20 yd Starts, Change of direction drills, Deceleration drills could arguably fit into this category as well (if you can slow down faster and in proper position it may improve the ability to accelerate faster)	200-400 yards
Max Velocity	Highest attainable velocity	20+ yard sprints	
Speed Endurance	Ability to maintain high velocity during a single sprint or repeated efforts	Longer sprints or multiple sprints	
Specific speed	Sport similar	Position drills	

The above information has detailed a hierarchy of athletic development. By developing a good base of work capacity, athletes are better prepared to handle the demands of more physically taxing loads further up the pyramid. Maintaining a simple plan allows athletes to learn and develop athletic qualities that are critical for the progression to more advanced levels of training and competitive play.

Layer 5 – Creating A Cultural Identity

Each organization should have a simple set of core beliefs/values used by the athletes, the coaches, and support staff to guide them through the daily operations. Adherence allows us to better problem solve, interact, and serve everyone in the organization. Here is an example of five simple expectations to help form a cultural identity:

1. Follow the Golden Rule (Treat others as you want to be treated)

- Respect everyone within the organization regardless of their responsibilities.

- Be fair, loyal and open minded, but stand firm for your beliefs.

- Avoid micromanagement by extending trust to individuals who demonstrate comfort within the system.

2. Be Disciplined

- Exhibit poise under pressure.

- Demonstrate character by maintaining a high level of detail throughout the calendar year.

- Maintain a high level of focus on important issues.

- Maintain a high standard of practice in the daily operations – especially the seemingly mundane.

3. Communicate effectively

- Use positive verbal and non-verbal social skills to connect with others.

- Information does not lead to behavior change - be dedicated to learning and teaching others with clarity.

- Be transparent, honest and tactful.

4. Be Relentless

- Persevere with consistent integrity - take pride in sacrifice and commitment.
- Perfect your craft by chasing expertise in your role.
- Mastery requires re-mastery.

5. No Excuses

- Maintain an uncommonly high level of concentration, consistency, craftsmanship.
- Be productive – find a way to finish the job regardless of what task you have been given.
- Be one step ahead - a lack of preparation by Party A does not constitute an emergency for Party B.
- "Any excuse, no matter how valid, only weakens the character" – Thomas S. Monson.

While processes may change over time, values will not. By providing a consistently high level of service, positive values will be instilled in our athletes, which will prove to be beneficial for their lifelong success. Additionally, adhering to these behaviors will apply the pressure of accountability in the unit while also providing a point of origin regarding expected behavior for those onboarding into the organization.

Layer 6 – Implementing The Cultural Plan

Implementing culture is all about relationships. In our profession, we are measured by the productivity of our athletes in all aspects of their lives. To help ensure their success, we must work to build relationships not only with our athletes, but everyone who has direct and indirect contact with them. The principles listed below will serve as a guide to achieve this.

<u>Demonstrate character and integrity</u>

- Lead by example: be a good role model.
- Work to build up each other after adversity (tough practice, game, criticism, etc.).
- Explain to those involved that we critique performance for improvement purposes and not to take such analysis personally.
- If we demand these things from our athletes we must require the same of ourselves.

<u>We must be great teachers</u>

- Find the best way to teach fundamentals, techniques and the 'why' to each individual.
- Keep it simple and ensure the audience is ready before progressing to advanced concepts.
- Utilize life's numerous teachable moments.
- Praise and critique everyone fairly.

<u>Meet in both team and individual settings</u>

- Assume the listener knows nothing – start from scratch.
- Be professional, prepared and have a plan.
- Have your audience come prepared to take notes (paper, pencil, etc.).
- Everyone must be team players and abide by rules and policies, especially those doing the teaching.

<u>Provide an environment the audience needs, not what you want</u>

- Display great enthusiasm, energy and be involved for the entirety of the session/practice/game/season within your responsibilities.
- Move and act with purpose: enthusiasm and intensity make deliberate practice contagious.
- All energy must be directed toward improvement while avoiding negativity.
- Everyone must be on time for every training session, workout or meeting.

- Be detailed and competitive in all aspects of your performance.
- Empower the audience and allow them to take responsibility and ownership.

<u>Develop self-starters and leaders</u>

- Foster the importance of team and encourage positive peer pressure.
- Promote the value of good work habits and principles of accountability.
- Constantly emphasize expectations: people perform better when they know the 'why'.

By professionally cultivating personal relationships within the organization through the above beliefs, we will surround each other with championship-level cohesiveness. This will allow us to use our influence to help everyone involved achieve their personal and professional goals.

Layer 7 – Assessing The Culture

At the end of the day our success is going to be evaluated by wins, losses and championships. Culture is undoubtedly a part of this, but it is a much more difficult metric to evaluate than a squat max, body composition, or range of motion. For this, perhaps the best measure would be the view from outside of the organization and/or those who are no longer a part of it:

- Are we an organization of which people want to be a part because of our ability to holistically develop talent?
- Do those who are no longer with us still come to team events, bring family and friends to facility, and promote the organization with pride?
- Do individuals speak positively of their time with us?
- Are our people sought after by other organizations because of their knowledge, talent, work ethic, and other job-related skills?

If the answer to these questions is "yes", then the organization has likely been successful in implementing a winning culture. To ensure this happens consistently, we need to be cognizant of when the answer is "no". Instead of being upset when this happens, use those occasions as opportunities for growth based on logic and performance. By using meticulous record-keeping, we can provide ourselves with an in-depth analysis of the operating policies and procedures we are using as our foundation. Consequently, we can identify and project successful trends and those needing alteration. We then put them into three different categories.

- Category 1 (Successful) - These services are currently operating with peak efficiency and have a positive effect on those we serve
- Category 2 (Need for Improvement) – These services are important enough to continue doing but we must look for ways to simplify, improve efficiency or reassign to different personnel
- Category 3 (Removal) – The resources spent providing these services would best be utilized elsewhere

By identifying the net effect of energy spent on tasks, we can decide which should be continued, delegated, removed or outsourced. This helps ensure we are putting our energy into those areas which are providing the best return on investment for our organization.

Summary

There are inevitable caveats to all of the information above, but at some point we must create a base for further progress and overcome inertia. Knowledge of development is not the same as development. Start simple, build upon your existing knowledge base, and never stop perfecting your craft. There is a lot of boring stuff that works, and it would be wise to start there. Whenever things start to become complicated, do not be afraid to use Occam's razor to cut through the excess.

Who is Andrew Althoff?

Andrew Althoff has worked at Baylor University since February 2009. Currently, he serves as Assistant AD for Sports Performance integrating the physical, psychological, and social aspects of student-athletes' performance into a practical approach for Baylor Athletics.

He currently holds a Master's in Education from Valdosta State University and a Bachelor's degree in Sports Science with minors in biology and coaching from Loras College. Additionally, he has certifications from the NSCA, The CSCCa, USA Weightlifting and is Functional Movement Certified.

9

Sport Science Data Infrastructure

A Primer for the Sports Practitioner

Landon Evans

Director of Sports Science

University of Iowa

I don't know about you, but I'm done engaging in the discussions where technology and data analysis comes into play within sport. They can be an incredible addition to the decision-making process. We know how complex certain situations may be, and in swimming through all the potential decision options we have, leveraging a thoughtful data environment can very much help that process. I've found this even truer when there are a lot of chefs in the kitchen. Sometimes, data and its respective analysis can cut through the emotional war rooms.

Where do you start? It can be very confusing. When you're entering a space in which you're not educated, you can feel you've been thrown into the deep end of the pool. To resolve your dilemma, some look to companies for the solutions, and specifically companies that are targeting sport. Companies are using a variety of tactics to sell you their products and services. Some are honest, some have poor taste. Fortunately, the publication space has done well here to help you and your team navigate what sort of technologies you can consider.

With more practitioners applying technology and collecting data these days, there has become a new bottleneck: data overload. Companies have listened and spun up solutions. This is where the athlete management systems have emerged. They can offer you solutions to aggregate your data from all of your sources, store it, and some suggest they can provide you instant analytical feedback so you can spend more time on your primary job responsibilities.

Athlete management systems have been applauded and criticized for a variety of reasons over the years. This isn't about discussing the pros and cons of using this type of service; rather, its aim is to give you a high-level overview of the generalized data pipeline. I believe detailing this for you and your organization can save you time and money. This chapter will go through some infrastructure considerations, options, and some of the specific design elements that make up our infrastructure at Iowa.

Why listen to me?

I have a good idea of who is picking up this book. I'm probably similar to you in many ways. I'm not an outsider. I'm in the weeds. But I'm not a full-time data engineer or data scientist. These areas are just a part of my job. So, why listen to me on this subject? Well, our group has data and technology scars. This has been a journey for sure. We've been at this for nearly seven years now. We have iterated over this process many times and continue to do so. But as of now, I can comfortably state we have embraced technology and data in a relatively balanced manner, not letting it sit on its own pedestal but allowing it to have a seat at the table. Make no mistake, we are humans. We like shiny objects and novelty just like anyone else. We've gone too far with it at times, and sometimes we simply didn't appreciate it enough. This will happen to you and your team as well.

Chapter scope

This is a high-level infrastructure chapter. It is not a data analysis chapter or a chapter on how to get people to buy into technology and data. However, let me make a couple comments on these two areas. From an analysis perspective, one of the best papers our group suggests to others to help see our perspective is, "To Explain or Predict" from Gailit Shmueli. She is a statistician but approaches the perspectives from a non-biased view. While it is hard to bucket our group into a camp, I'll just state we are more biased towards a Bayesian perspective in many cases and we have been very influenced by the options and our respective outcomes from machine and deep learning approaches.

Regarding culture, we have a wonderful group at Iowa. Our administration, coaches, support staff, and most importantly, our student-athletes have been through the ups and downs in a variety of situations. Technology and data have been a part of some of those ups and downs. We have learned a lot over the years and continue to do so. In spite of this, technology and data over time have essentially been baked into most of our teams' workflows. This has taken time, but it wouldn't have been possible without the people we have at Iowa.

Technical Jargon

I am fortunate to have a computing background. When I come across a technological roadblock, I generally know at least where to look for a solution. This is sometimes more than half the battle. Fortunately, I'm assuming that most reading this are coming from the human performance background so some of the vernacular may be hard to follow, but I'm making a conscious effort keeping the technical jargon to a minimum. With that said, some terms may be impossible to leave out. Don't worry. Don't let the vernacular intimidate you.

Why Consider Infrastructure Design?

If you're new to technology and data for sport, this may seem like a chapter you could easily skip. Perhaps you're a strength coach or physical therapist that believes this is out of your scope or even responsibilities to understand. You may be right and by all means, I'd probably consider skipping it too if I was in your situation. However, its 2019 and technology and data have been a part of the sporting landscape for quite some time and its involvement (for better or worse) is rapidly increasing. It's inevitable you'll need to engage with technology and data at some point within your career. Even if this isn't within your scope or responsibilities, in my opinion, it's important to broaden your scope to understand areas that may impact your environment.

As with anything entering into your environment, it can change the dynamics of how factors operate. When a new hire comes into your organization or a new piece of technology is added, both can alter the whole entity. So, it may be wise to consider your framework for the future growth of these changes. Ultimately, it can give you an appreciation for the possible solutions to allow the data journey from acquisition to report to effective implementation.

Where to start?

Before you start considering the infrastructure for your environment, you should consider your current situation and the people around you. Here is a short list of questions to consider if you're starting from scratch or trying to improve on what you're already doing.

- How technically savvy are you and your co-workers? If you are and your coworkers are not, think about the educational time requirements here. What if no one is? Skill up or lean on others? Do you have the time? How about the ROI on skilling up?

- Can you make a new hire to steer and manage this? This may be a better ROI than you or your colleagues to up-skill themselves.

- Do you have a supportive Information Technology (IT) department? Will they help with shared hardware and software infrastructure costs? How willing are they to up-skill themselves in an area that you want to leverage but they don't possess requisite knowledge? How open are they with new systems integrating into their network? Security considerations?

- How embedded are current services and technologies already in place at your organization? If your medical staff has an electronic medical record (EMR) system they've been using for many years, should you convince them to abandon it for something else?

- Budget? Can you buy into an athlete management system? What if you do that but now you don't have any funds to purchase other equipment that can generate other datasets that you find valuable? What can you purchase now and what can wait until the next fiscal year?

- Who on the team will be the principal lead? If this person leaves, can the infrastructure still operate?

- Open Source vs. Closed Source options. While open source is free and most great open source projects have wonderful support and communities, there may be a larger cost of ownership with free solutions. The concept of Total Cost of Ownership needs to be considered.

- Your community. Anyone around that can help support your efforts? Physiology, Biomechanics, Statistics, Computer Science, Engineering departments at your school or local schools? Undergraduate students that have a senior project or in-the-field volunteer responsibilities?

- On-premise vs. cloud? How much security of the data is required for you and your organization?

Many of your answers to questions such as these should drive a large segment of your implementation decisions. If you have a minimal technical background and no other support members to pick up that limitation for you and your group, you may be in the market for athlete management systems or excel-based 'database/dashboard' solutions. However, if you have a supportive IT department, good technical know-how, and are wanting a more modular-based infrastructure, then you may consider a 'make your own' solution. There are so many possible arrangements here. So, let's describe some of the possible items you may consider within your infrastructure. These specific items can be categorically placed under five different labels: **Data Acquisition**, **Data Post Processing**, **Data Storage**, **Data Modeling / Visualization**, and **Data Publishing**.

Data Acquisition

All subsequent steps depend on this, so it is quite arguably the most important area. You want actionable insight from data? First, you need to start with good data. This is sourced from valid and reliable tools that have a standard operating procedure behind them. Still, the chapter isn't about those tools. Most readers here have a good idea of what those could be: physiology devices to player tracking systems to subjective wellness information to medical data. A lot of options exist here. However, let us spend a moment discussing things that don't get mentioned enough.

Standard operating procedures

Standard operating procedures (SOP) are detailed documents that are your checklists of operation. This is your stepwise documented solution that everyone in the organization follows to ensure the data acquisition is done correctly. These documents also can quickly summarize the purpose of the assessment, pertinent metrics, and so forth. For example, for Omegawave, our SOP outlines the steps to setup our student-athletes with software and hardware. Additionally, there are instructions detailing the manner in which the athlete should test with their mobile device.

Service Testing of Hardware

This is the boring part of owning hardware. It would be wonderful to buy hardware and it would simply work, and forever. But ... it doesn't. You need to spend time ensuring your hardware is still providing you what you hope it's providing you. For example, if you own force plates, calibration usually requires an outside scale company or an engineering group to do this. Yet even just using simple calibrated external weights and placing them directly in the middle of the plate should provide you that at least your athlete's weights are being captured correctly. This isn't perfect but it is helpful. While keeping with force plates, if you use portable plates, if you have dust accumulating under the feet, it can cause some noise in your data. Keep things clean!

Additionally, GPS units have been criticized about various metrics, but companies may claim a different story. Exercise caution and test devices yourself. I distinctly remember one of our devices being off by 25% of a known distance when tested. That isn't good! Still, the companies don't know when their hardware is getting worse. You need to test and objectively show them. Most companies are good, and they will assist you with replacements.

Data Post Processing

We've collected our data, but now we need to do something with it. This is where I'll introduce the concept of Extract, Transform, Load (ETL) to those non-technical folks. This is the process in which you take data from one source and copy it to another source (e.g. database).

Extract

This term accurately conveys the process. We are extracting the data from the source. The two primary ways are direct export or by an online storage site. With direct export, you're likely engaging with a piece of software that is interfacing to a piece of hardware. For instance, if you are using accelerometer devices, you're quite possibly plugging them into your computer or via ANT+ or Bluetooth. The respective software gives you the option to download the data off said device. This is usually saved in a comma-separated values (CSV) file format or even an Excel file. It's usually ideal if companies provide a CSV file, as it's easy to move this data file across many different programs that may, natively by default, use different formats (e.g. databases, spreadsheets, text editors).

The problem with the manual extraction method is that it can be slow and requires a human, and humans are prone to making errors. A common occurrence that we encountered was that one of our manual exporting tasks was generating a CSV file. On some occasions the person in charge would open the file and it would default into Microsoft Excel. Excel will automatically do things to your data without you realizing it. As an example, it will change a date field of YY-MM-DD to Y-MM-DD. This can halt your loading process into a database. To further clarify Excel and its issues, Christopher Ingraham wrote an article appearing in the Washington Post titled: "An Alarming Number of Scientific Papers Contain Excel Errors", which serves as an outstanding quick reference.

The other way to extract your data is by accessing an online repository that may or may not have a software frontend to access it. Concerning GPS data, typically when the devices are plugged into their charging docks this is configured to sync the data into the computer and then out to an online repository. In this instance, GPS systems allow you to extract data locally off that specific computer, but it seems most access it online. From here, you have a couple options to retrieve the data. One is manual, and the other two are automated. The first option mirrors the direct export, but you're interfacing with a web front-end to download the data you wish. Again, the process is manual.

The other methods are automated. The first one is accessing the data that lives online by an application program interface (API). This word is an umbrella term for many types of uses, but simply, it is the ability for (in our case) a server to receive requests by users or programs and send back responses. In our case, we would be sending the request for data with the hope it will return back what we want. This is what companies are talking about when they tell you they have an API available. This can make the process quite manageable. To gain access to these APIs, you'll usually need to get some information from the company so you can authorize yourself appropriately. Forewarning though: some companies may charge to get access to their API.

While there are many tools, some great free options are: **PostMan** (www.getpostman.com), **Requests** (2.python-requests.org), and **httr** (httr.r-lib.org). Postman is a graphical user interface application that is available for Mac, Windows, and Linux. This may be your first sandbox experience with APIs. This is where I will test API calls before I write them in code. With code, I exclusively use the Python programming language for this and leverage the **Requests** library. I have experience with **httr** in R, but I prefer the Python ecosystem in these instances.

With these tools, you can now call these APIs and capture the data you wish. Calling these APIs now makes it possible to set up the system so that it is known what you want and when these programs or libraries up to allow the ability to get the data you want in a scheduled manner. For instance, with our Omegawave data, we request data from the Omegawave API every 15 minutes from 5:30 AM to 12:00 PM every day.

However, let's say your company doesn't have an API but has a web interface that can give you access to extract the data. This is where web scraping enters the process.

Before I explain, you need to understand the terms of service with the automation of data collection. In the past, people have been sued for web scraping. This likely won't ever happen to you, but just do your due diligence by reading the company's terms of service regarding how you can engage with their website.

With web scraping, you can programmatically automate the data extraction from these websites that have no API available. For instance, if you want to gather all of your baseball team's statistics from publicly available websites and put it into a useable format, you are able to do. The two tools that I use are **Requests** in Python and **RVest** (rvest.tidyverse.org) in R. The additional layers you need to understand a bit more on is HTML, CSS, and usually some Javascript. It is not necessary to grasp how to program these yourself, but to follow the structure of how things are generally working. There are a number of great tutorials online to help with this. Ultimately, you can programmatically authenticate yourself to a website and download the data you wish.

Transform

The next step is to transform your data. Sometimes the data you extract is already in the format you want. The data with which we are typically working is in a tabular format which is simply rows and columns. Unfortunately, companies persist on putting excessive information in these datasets. This will yield untidy data.

Tidy data is defined by https://r4ds.had.co.nz/tidy-data.html

1. Each variable must have its own column.

2. Each observation must have its own row.

3. Each value must have its own cell.

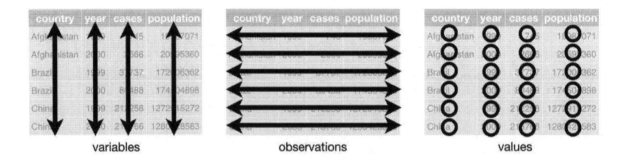

The great aspect about this format is that doing any sort of analysis is tremendously easier. Also, from that point, you can continue to transform the data however you wish when you're in the analysis mode. Still, for the means of preparing the data to eventually load it into an aggregated area where your other datasets live is critical to consider how it will be transformed. I recommend the tidy way. I wish companies would too.

When you are calling data from an API, it is commonly in a JavaScript Object Notation (JSON) format. This is a very readable format, but it is not tidy-ready. You'll generally need to study it to understand its 'tree' illustrating how the data is organized. Here is an example of Omegawave JSON output.

```
{
  "GUID": "REMOVED",
  "SubjectGUID": "REMOVED",
  "Name": "REMOVED",
  "AssessmentDateTime": "2019-03-02T12:50:08.5Z",
  "AssessmentDateTimeInLocalTime": "2019-03-02T06:50:08.5Z",
  "Modified": "2019-03-02T12:54:46.3875259Z",
  "TimezoneOffsetMins": -360,
  "GenesisIndexModified": "2019-03-02T12:54:46.3875259Z",
  "Disabled": false,
  "CalculationStatusGenesis": "OK",
  "AssessmentTags": [
    {
      "TagValue": "",
      "TagName": "AssessmentTagBefore",
      "Modified": "2019-03-02T12:54:45.623Z",
      "LinkedObjectGUID": "REMOVED"
    }
  ],
  "FirstName": "REMOVED",
  "LastName": "REMOVED",

  "Indexes": [
    {
      "Value": "5",
      "ValueType": "Int16",
      "Name": "GenesisAdaptationReservesGrade"
    },
    {
      "Value": "False",
      "ValueType": "Boolean",
      "Name": "GenesisHighArrythmia"
    },
    {
      "Value": "0.68",
      "ValueType": "Floating",
      "Name": "GenesisPNS"
    },
    {
      "Value": "67",
      "ValueType": "Floating",
      "Name": "RestingHR"
    },
    {
      "Value": "3",
      "ValueType": "Int16",
      "Name": "GenesisRank1"
    }
```

At this point, this information will need to be transformed. Unfortunately, I've never used a GUI tool to do this, so I have no suggestions in this case. In Python, I still would recommend **Requests** since it has a built-in JSON method or the separate **JSON** library. In R, I've used **JSONLITE** with success. These can help you parse the JSON data so you can write it to a CSV file.

Load

You've acquired, you've transformed it, now you're ready to load the data into its permanent home. If you have a database, this is where you can now directly write your new data to the appropriate table. If not, then you may consider appending your new data to an existing dataset. For instance, if you're pulling down daily HRV data, you're not going to want to have files for each day. So, appending to a single file makes sense. Again, this is where coding is convenient with just a couple lines of code. In Python, I prefer the **Pandas** library. In R, my choice is the **dplyr** library. When writing to a database, I use **Pandas** and **SQLAlchemy** when in Python. In R, I've used **ODBC**. Most of these tools to write to a database work with multiple relational databases like SQL Server, MySQL, PostgreSQL, etc. I'm not aware if they write to non-relational databases.

Data Storage

You've acquired your data. You've performed the necessary extract and transform steps, but not necessarily the load step. We briefly spoke on it, here in the domain of Data Storage, there need to be some considerations of your data's home.

First, there are many different types of digital media. The primary ones you'll possibly utilize are text, video, and images. Let's quickly discuss video and images.

With video and images, while you can store these into databases, it is generally a poor option. The better practice is to have a set storage container for items such as this, for instance a network drive or a simple storage service (S3). Then you will store metadata or at minimum at least the URI/URL into the database. The popular S3 option is **Amazon S3**. Other options are **B2** from Backblaze, **Spaces** by Digital Ocean, **Microsoft Azure Blob**, and **Google Cloud Storage**. In some instances, people will leverage video storage solutions directly that have a suite of software built into a web-frontend. Examples here are **Dartfish**, **Hudl**, and **Sportscode**.

On the text side, this is what you classically think is your 'data'. Storage for this type of media is either local files (Excel, CSV, proprietary formats), network LAN storage, cloud storage, or databases. Be aware that you don't necessarily have to pick just one. In fact, we use all of these options. Additionally, having redundancy built in is wise as hardware fails, someone accidentally deletes data, or some other mishap causes your data to be destroyed.

Still, in best practice, it is wise to aggregate your datasets to a database. This provides multiple benefits besides simple aggregation. They can scale very well, they can handle very large data sets, and you can quickly build our relationships between data tables with JOINS. There are a lot more benefits of using a database, but that is beyond the scope of this chapter. Ultimately, having a certain home gives you and the organization an authoritative version of the data. That then enables everyone to be viewing and analyzing from the same data as everyone else.

There are two types of databases: relational and non-relational. Relational databases have structure and work in arrangements called tables. These tables are made up of data that has columns and rows. In non-relational databases, data isn't necessarily structured but provides a flexibility of what is input and how it is stored. There are pros and cons of each type. For most of you reading this, I suggest you should consider a relational database because most of the datasets you're likely using are in a structured manner. Additionally, if you would want to perform JOINS between tables (e.g. Wellness Data table with HRV table), you'll need a relational database. Popular databases are **SQL Server**, **MySQL**, **PostgreSQL**, **Oracle**, etc. We personally use SQL Server, but I have experience with both MySQL and PostgreSQL, and both have worked well for my use cases.

Data Modeling and Visualization

At this point, the fun begins for most people. You want to produce some tricked out visualization that will force lead boss to give you a raise. While I appreciate your enthusiasm, let us pump the breaks and layout two key sections here.

Those two sections are interactive querying and visualization.

Interactive Querying

In the last 10 years, there has been a sharp presence of computational programming in sport. The tools including **Excel**, **SPSS**, **RapidMiner**, **SAS**, **Matlab**, and **Graphpad Prism** have been bullied by open source options in the R and Python communities. Both R and Python have rich data analysis options and with the rise of both languages, there are a plethora of educational resources. However, if you're not interested in programming to derive your analysis, there are great open source tools that are GUIs. Tools such as **JASP** (jasp-stats.org) and **Jamovi** (www.jamovi.org) are wonderful choices.

If you want to directly connect to your database though, I'm not aware of options through JASP and Jamovi. Within Python, **pyodbc** and **SQLAlchemy** are great libraries. Within R, the libraries **odbc** with **DBI** work well.

When you're directly connected to your database now through Python or R, you can easily begin exploring the data to start uncovering some potential answers to your questions. While I currently spend most of my time in Python, I've learned much from viewing David Robinson's Tidy Tuesday screencasts on YouTube. He performs various analysis on datasets he has never before seen and thus reveals a raw look into his exploratory process.

Visualization

Continuing with the common theme of this chapter, let's consider a high-level look at where visualization may fit into the entire data pipeline. There are many reasons to visualize your data, but the common example used to illustrate the possible need is the *Anscombe Quartet*.

Below you have four different data sets that provide some similar statistical properties.

	I		II		III		IV	
	x	y	x	y	x	y	x	y
	10	8,04	10	9,14	10	7,46	8	6,58
	8	6,95	8	8,14	8	6,77	8	5,76
	13	7,58	13	8,74	13	12,74	8	7,71
	9	8,81	9	8,77	9	7,11	8	8,84
	11	8,33	11	9,26	11	7,81	8	8,47
	14	9,96	14	8,1	14	8,84	8	7,04
	6	7,24	6	6,13	6	6,08	8	5,25
	4	4,26	4	3,1	4	5,39	19	12,5
	12	10,84	12	9,13	12	8,15	8	5,56
	7	4,82	7	7,26	7	6,42	8	7,91
	5	5,68	5	4,74	5	5,73	8	6,89
SUM	99,00	82,51	99,00	82,51	99,00	82,50	99,00	82,51
AVG	9,00	7,50	9,00	7,50	9,00	7,50	9,00	7,50
STDEV	3,32	2,03	3,32	2,03	3,32	2,03	3,32	2,03

When visualized though, some clear differences are readily apparent.

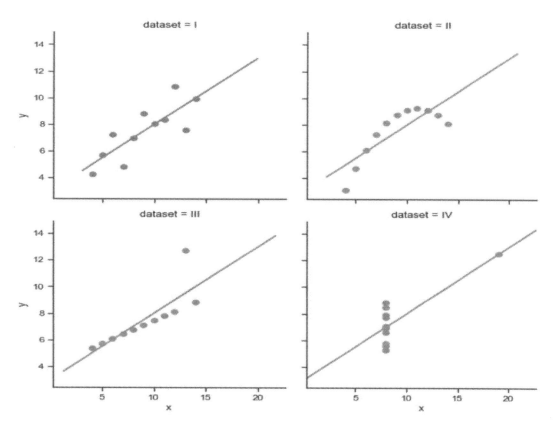

Remember that other statistical tests can be employed to find these differences, but that isn't necessarily the point. Besides telling an improved story through a visual medium, visualizing data can help you quickly explore your data as well.

The common libraries people use in Python are **Matplotlib**, **Seaborn**, **Bokeh**, **Plotly**, **Plotnine**, and **Altair**. In R, you typically see people use **ggplot** and **Plotly**. As with most topics, people have wildly different opinions on which library is best in the Python and R worlds. I'll share with you that when I'm in R, it's 100% probable I'd be using ggplot. It is a wonderful library and integrated well with other data science libraries. When I'm in Python, I largely prefer Altair and Seaborn.

However, these require coding. If you don't want to code, you can leverage built-in visualizations in your graphical statistical software, or you can leverage business intelligence software packages such as **Microsoft PowerBI**, and **Tableau**. These tools have drag and drop capabilities to build out visualizations very easily. This is how most athlete management systems operate with their visualization features.

Data Publishing

You're almost there. It is time to think about how your stack-holders are going to ingest your analysis and visualizations. Are your analysis and visualizations only for you? Do they need to be shared with a small group? How about a large group? How do they prefer to ingest their information? Do they want it delivered to their inbox, or do they want to login to a system where everything lives because their inbox is a blackhole?

In terms of options, continue to think about the future with all of your decisions. Consider how people are ingesting information these days and see if your solution is compatible with those methods. Visual analysis that stays on my local machine is done often and is for my viewing only. There are moments when I'll simply quickly shoot a rendered report to someone's inbox. Yet, when there is constant data coming in from the same sources or there is a large analysis required, employing interactive visualizations can greatly help here. The reason why they can be helpful is it can give the end-user some control of how and what they are seeing. They can explore the data in a manner that may make more sense to them. There can be some negative consequences to this, but all options have two sides of their respective coin.

Numerous interactive options can also be deployed to a centralized home where the end-users can point their mobile device or computer to a web URL and begin ingesting the information. Common options that seem present in the sports space are **Shiny**, **Dash**, **Tableau**, and **PowerBI**.

Athlete Management Systems vs Make Your Own

I've made some mentions of athlete management systems that can be a part of the infrastructure solution. The biggest selling points for athlete management systems are they can help you aggregate most of your data sets, make some of the manual data entry process simplified, and the cost has everything else incorporated (e.g. hardware costs, bandwidth, support). These factors can greatly benefit a myriad of people and organizations.

While athlete management systems are popular, I would like to comment on a couple items people should at least be aware of.

I have two primary concerns with athlete management systems. First is a cautionary point about how some of these systems are now providing tons of options. Workout builders, EMR (electronic medical records) systems, communication platforms, and much more are frequently available. While they are great at what they provide, so many places already have many of these platforms set up and are deeply integrated into the workflows of numerous users. Centralizing every aspect into a single platform may perhaps have value. The biggest challenge is to draw large numbers of people into making these changes. Additionally, there are resources required to ensure all of these tools are of high quality. This prioritization of their time isn't for you to control. If you have a service request change, this may take weeks, months, or sometimes it may not happen at all. You're not the only person or organization they are serving.

Second, and from my experience, the analytical tooling is weak. Of course, you can create alert systems based on self-selected rules, basic descriptive statistic reports, and some satisfactory visualization options. However, deeper data analysis, modeling, and impactful visualizations are hard to attain. Some are surely providing a simple way to connect to their databases so more sophisticated tooling can be leveraged, but suppose you wish to put your model into production immediately? Imagine that you want to create a rich interactive visual for your stockholders. This is where I feel athlete management systems are truly only capturing Data Acquisition, Data Post Processing, and Data Storage. The last two components, Data Modeling and Visualization, and Data Publishing are suffering.

Our Infrastructure

A picture is frequently all that is needed to see how this could all be consolidated. Below is a network diagram of our current infrastructure at Iowa. This will continue to evolve, but it is set up to accommodate those changes when they come. Additionally, we have chosen certain hardware and software because of our IT department and security considerations (e.g. on-premise SQL and Tableau server).

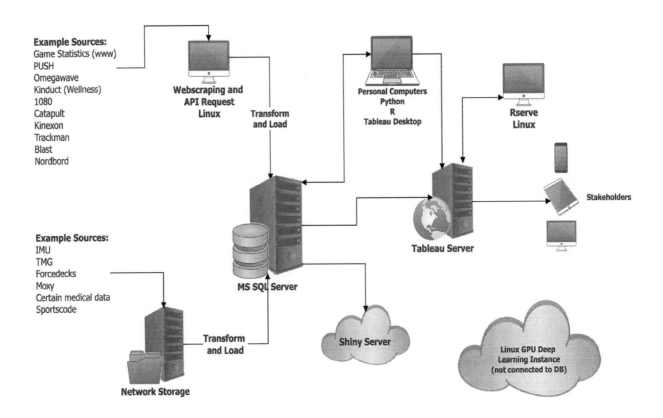

Conclusion

You made it! So many things to consider, and amazingly, we omitted topics such as data governance, organizational software standards, language support, code versioning, debugging, hardware considerations, and much more. Yet, if this is your first time seeing the big picture, I hope I've left the impression that you should consider infrastructure design when examining your data environment for the present and future.

Who is Landon Evans?

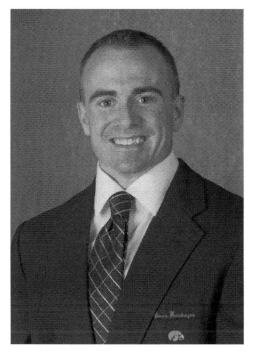

Landon Evans director of sports science in the Department of Athletics at the University of Iowa; a strength & conditioning coach for the track & field program; and an active research member with the Virtual Soldier Research program within the College of Engineering. He has also served as the sports nutrition coordinator for the Department of Athletics.

Evans received a Bachelor of Science in Health & Human Performance from Iowa State in 2005, a Master of Science in Kinesiology and Recreation from Illinois State in 2007 and DPD Concentration in Family & Consumer Sciences, with emphasis on food, nutrition and dietetics from Illinois State 2011.

He is a Registered Dietitian (RD), Certified Strength and Conditioning Specialist (CSCS) from the National Strength and Conditioning Association, Strength & Conditioning Coach Certified (SCCC) through the Collegiate Strength & Conditioning Coaches Association. He is CPR/AED certified.

10

Sleep and Adaptation

Dr. Erik Korem

Associate Athletics Director for Student-Athlete High Performance
College of William and Mary

Preface

My interest in sleep and its relationship to sports performance grew from the nagging question that all performance coaches ask themselves, "What else?" What else can I be doing to help my athletes? What else should I add or take away from my programming to achieve a greater training effect? It wasn't until 2012, when I started working with Omegawave technology, that I began asking a new set of questions. How do I create an environment of optimal adaptability for my athletes? Maybe it's not *what* I am doing, but rather in *what* context are the means/methods being applied and how is that related to the realization of the training effect?

This line of questioning led me to the phenomenon of sleep. I reasoned that there were only a few things that human beings needed to survive: food, water and sleep (fatal insomnia). Therefore, if optimal nutrition, hydration, and sleep were present in the training process then the full effect of any training intervention could be realized. Now let me take a moment to make very clear that this isn't an endorsement of the "anything works" model of thinking. We all know the coaches that say, "there a million ways to skin a cat", and usually those are the lazy types. If you are reading this manual it's most likely because you are of the minority that believes that reverse engineering performance and developing target-specific programs are the only way to optimize the training process…I digress. The intent of this chapter is to create awareness of precisely how critical sleep is to the training process, and to provide the reader with some practical tools for improving sleep and therefore training ability of your athletes.

As the English dramatist Thomas Dekker wrote "Sleep is the golden chain that ties health and our bodies together" (1). During my doctoral studies, I learned that sleep is an essential biological process (2) that is required for the human organism to grow, adapt (3) and thrive (4, 5). Sleep is also considered a necessity for both cognitive and physiological function (3) and is posited to play a critical role in recovery from exercise (6). In addition, sleep is consistently regarded as the most efficacious strategy for improving recovery to enhance sport performance (7,8). The literature demonstrates a reciprocal relationship between sleep quantity versus exercise and sport performance (9-16) thus making it a topic of great interest in the sports science community (17).

Occurring at consistent intervals during a 24-hour period, the sleep state is marked by reduced motor activity, fluctuations in body temperature, hormonal activity, eye movement, muscle tone, electroencephalograph (EEG) oscillations (18) and regional brain activity (3). From a behavioral context, sleep can be defined as "a homeostatically regulated state of reduced movement and sensory responsiveness" (19). Despite our understanding of the order and synchrony of sleep, a single locus of control has yet to be identified (2). A specific anatomical landmark has yet to be identified that when lesioned can completely eliminate sleep. Thus, sleep in some ways still remains a mystery in the biological sciences, and because of its ambiguous nature, it should be viewed as a "broad system-wide phenomenon" without a locus of complete control (2,20).

Performance in any sport is more than the expression of physical output, rather it is a compilation of physical, psychological, technical, and tactical components working together to execute a motor task. These components are affected by fluctuations in behavioral and physiological processes across a 24-hour period in a rhythmic pattern. These rhythms are generated by circadian clocks, which are considered to be the internal time-keeping machinery of biological systems (20). Circadian clocks are dependent upon cyclic environmental cues called zeitgebers, which is German for time givers. Zeitgebers such as light, temperature, and humidity can alter or reset the timing or phase of circadian rhythmicity (21). Zeitgebers prevent "free running" of endogenous rhythms by entraining them to a 24-hour rhythm (22).

Any process that repeats itself every 24-hours and persists in the absence of external time cues is considered to be a circadian rhythm (23). In mammals, circadian rhythms are controlled by the suprachiasmatic nucleus (SCN) which is found in the anterior hypothalamus (24-26). The SCN exerts limited control over the sleep-wake cycle, as humans are highly sensitive to changes in their environment. This is an important consideration when planning team travel as even small fluctuations in room temperature, noise and ambient lighting can have a significant impact upon athletes experiencing restful and restorative sleep.

Although the timing of normative sleep is constrained to a specific portion of a 24-hour day, nocturnal sleep duration is largely under volitional control (e.g., staying up late, 6am workouts) with circadian modifiers playing a significant role in sleep duration. Alexander Borbely developed the two-process model of sleep regulation, which is a quantitative model that describes alternation of human sleep and wakefulness as the interaction of circadian and homeostatic processes (22, 24, 27, 28). The two-process model consists of a homeostatic process (process S) which represents our need or drive for sleep, and a circadian process (process C) which is controlled by the SCN. It has been proposed that process C sets limits on process S, but these limits fluctuate with the time of day. Wakefulness is initiated when the homeostatic drive for sleep reaches its lower limit and sleep is initiated when the homeostatic drive reaches its upper limit.

As I studied the literature I found that the regulation of sleep by homeostatic and circadian processes has a much broader scope of influence than just initiating sleep or wakefulness. Van Dongen and Dinges state, "The biological clock also modulates our hour-to-hour waking behavior, as reflected in fatigue, alertness, and performance, generating circadian rhythmicity in almost all neurobehavioral variables" (21). Research indicates that there may be a circadian influence on athletic performance. According to Drust et al. (29), an examination of world record-breaking performances reveals a circadian variation with these performances occurring in the early evening, which coincides with a peak in body temperature (29). Thun et al. (22) state that: "Performance is better in the afternoon or evening than in the morning for nearly all kinds of sports demanding physical skills. Technical performance may peak some-what earlier in the day than skills demanding more power." Circadian influence on performance has yet to be fully elucidated, but the current literature suggests that it should be considered in preparation for individual and team performance.

In addition to the homeostatic and circadian process, there is an ultradian (shorter than a day but longer than an hour) process that occurs within sleep. The ultradian process is composed of two alternating sleep states: rapid eye movement (REM) sleep and non-rapid eye movement (NREM) sleep (30). For a healthy young adult on a fixed sleep routine, the normal pattern of sleep consists of 90 to 110-minute cycles of sleep divided into NREM and REM sleep (31). NREM sleep is proposed to assist in energy conservation (32), tissue repair (33) and nervous system recuperation (3). During NREM sleep, the largest 24-hour pulse of growth hormone (GH) is released from the pituitary gland (34). GH is an anabolic hormone that plays a critical role in bone building (35), muscle hypertrophy (36) and mobilization of free fatty acids (37), all of which are critical for the adaptive processes associated with training. REM sleep is proposed to play a critical role in emotional regulation, localized recuperative processes (38), testosterone secretion, and memory consolidation (18).

Although the literature is incomplete regarding the impact of sleep on the various physiological systems, there is a wealth of evidence to suggest that sleep plays a critical role in immune (39) and endocrine function (40) as well as disease states. Recently, Watson and colleagues (39) demonstrated that when genetic factors are controlled for (healthy monozygotic twin pairs), habitual short sleep durations are linked to gene down regulation across functionally diverse categories including immune responses, which may be related to negative metabolic, cardiovascular and inflammatory outcomes. Spiegel et al. (40) determined that six-nights of sleep restriction negatively impacted endocrine function (decreased thyrotropin concentrations), heart rate variability (increased sympathovagal tone) and impaired carbohydrate metabolism.

Restricted sleep is also considered a risk factor for numerous types of cancer. Sleeping 3 to 5 hours a night has been shown to increase the risk of dying from prostate cancer by 55% for men younger than 65 years of age (41). In 2007, the International Agency for Research on Cancer, a part of the World Health Organization, categorized shift work as a group 2A carcinogen, which places in it a similar risk category as ultraviolet radiation and acrylamide (42). Short sleep durations ($\leq$ 6 hr.) are associated with an increased risk for metabolic syndrome, and in a recent meta-analysis a u-shaped dose-response relationship was observed between sleep quantity and the risk of type 2 diabetes (43).

Sleep durations between 7-8 hours were found to be the lowest risk category. Finally, the findings of a 2017 study with 500 adults over 19 years of age investigating the relationship between sleep and metabolic syndrome, glucose and lipid metabolism, and inflammation, found a negative association between sleep duration and BMI and waist circumference (44). In addition, a positive association was found for sleep duration and high-density lipo-protein (HDL) cholesterol. These studies support the growing body of research that indicates that sleep plays a critical role in disease states.

Consistent and fulfilling sleep has long been associated with memory consolidation and learning. During my doctoral studies, I found that there exists a comprehensive body of research from a wide range of neuroscientific disciplines (45), which are complemented by cellular and molecular models of sleep-dependent plasticity (46), to support sleep-dependent memory processing (47). Robert Stickgold describes memory consolidation as a long-term process following initial memory encoding that includes "a series of cellular, molecular and systems-level alterations" (18). These alterations develop over time and stabilize and enhance the initial memory, outside our conscious awareness and without additional practice. Sleep dependent memory consolidation implies that for most tasks, consolidation is most significant during sleep (off-line) compared to wake (on-line) (48).

There is a substantial amount of cellular and molecular evidence to support the role of sleep in promoting brain plasticity (49). According to Tononi and Cirelli "sleep is the price the brain pays for plasticity" (50). Tononi and Cirelli developed the synaptic homeostasis hypothesis (SHY) which proposes that the "fundamental function of sleep is the restoration of synaptic homeostasis, which is challenged by synaptic strengthening triggered by learning during wake and synaptogenesis during development" (50). Essentially, if there wasn't a sleep state, which allows for homeostatic regulation, synaptic depression and potentiation would lead to an obliteration or oversaturation of neural signaling and mental traces. Recently, de Vivo et al. (47) confirmed that synaptic scaling occurred during sleep states in mouse motor and sensory cortices underscoring the critical function that sleep serves in the dynamic process of brain plasticity. In addition, Wang and colleagues (51) recently found that phosphorylation of sleep-need-indexed phosphoproteins (SNIPP) accumulate and dissipate in relation to sleep needs in mice.

SNIPP phosphorylation is now considered to represent a molecular signature for the sleep need and is thought to represent a primary regulatory mechanism that underlies both sleep-wake homeostasis and synaptic homeostasis (51). In brief, have you ever had a "foggy brain" after not getting enough sleep? This may be the reason why!

Although sleep is considered the most effective recovery strategy for elite athletes, there is not a consensus regarding sleep quantity recommendations. Bompa and Haff (52) suggest that athletes require 9 to 10 hours of sleep, with 80-90% being obtained at night. The National Sleep Foundation recommends 7 to 9 hours of nocturnal sleep for young adults (ages 18-25 yr.). Despite these recommendations, the literature suggests that athletes sleep far less than what may be considered optimal for training and performance (3).

Mah and colleagues (53) recently examined the sleep duration and quality of over 600 athletes across 29 sports at Stanford University. 42.4% of the cohort was identified as being poor sleepers with sleep durations of <7 hours being reported by 39% of the athletes, and 59% of the teams averaging <7 hours a night during the week. Also, 51% of the athletes indicated high levels of daytime sleepiness. Mah et al. concluded that "collegiate athletes generally experience poor sleep quality, habitually obtain insufficient sleep, and experience substantial daytime sleepiness" (53). In another study of 130 Division 1 collegiate athletes, 43% of the student-athletes were found to sleep <6 hours during weekdays and 15% reported sleeping <6 hours on weekends.

The follow-up question to this data should be, "How does sleep duration effect exercise and sport performance"? The answer provides a mixed bag. Studies investigating the relationship between sleep loss, deprivation and restriction and exercise performance have yielded conflicting results. Fullagar et al. (3) state the following:

> *"These varied results are mainly attributed to differences in exercise protocols, participants' fitness, and the experimental environment. For instance, variations in thermoregulatory responses, habituation to sleep loss and the time of day at which activities are performed have a complex interaction with exerciseperformance, and thus, may potentially mask the effect of sleep loss."*

Therefore, caution should be applied when examining the relationship between sleep loss and exercise performance.

There is literature that suggests that sleep restriction and deprivation can lead to decrements in endurance, speed, strength, power as well as expressions of sport-specific skill (69, 54). It has been reported that altered perception of effort may account for negative changes in endurance performance following total sleep deprivation (55). The work of Goel et al. (56) complements this finding, wherein they found that under sleep deprived conditions, "Increased compensatory effort is required to remain behaviorally effective". Therefore, sleep loss may affect performance despite equivalent applied efforts (54). From a practical standpoint, this may account for a disconnect between a coach and athlete's perception of effort.

Skein et al. (57) found that 30 hours of total sleep deprivation (SD) negatively impacted intermittent-sprint performance, reduced mean sprint times, and SD led to an elevation of negative mood states and a suppression of positive feelings. *As a side note, I love it when the literature supports what coaches already know!* Skein and colleagues suggest that SD may affect intermittent-sprint performance through integrated afferent feedback from the periphery. They propose that reduced muscle glycogen and increased perceptual strain may reduce recruitment of active musculature (57). Takeuchi et al. (58) found that 64 hours of total SD did not affect 40-meter sprint times; however, vertical jump height was significantly reduced. Finally, Blumert et al. (59) studied the effects of 24 hours of total SD on weightlifting performance and mood states with national-caliber male weightlifters. Total SD did not affect maximal weight lifted in the front squat, clean and jerk, or snatch exercises. However, a Profile of Mood States (POMS) questionnaire revealed significant changes in fatigue, confusion, vigor and total mood disturbance. The authors concluded that "If an athlete is in an acute period of sleep loss, as noticed by negative mood disturbances, it may be more beneficial to focus on the psychological (motivation) rather than the physiological aspect of the sport" (59).

Sleep loss has been demonstrated to negatively impact sport specific skill and performance. A mere four hours of sleep restriction (SR) negatively impacts hand-eye coordination, evidenced by changes in accuracy and variability in dart throwing (60). Dart players missed the target more frequently and were less accurate, and this decrement in performance was interpreted as a general deterioration in psychomotor performance (60,61).

Sleep restriction has been demonstrated to reduce serving accuracy with semi-professional tennis players; whereas sleep extension by 2 hours per night improved serving accuracy in Division III tennis players (62,63). Additionally, in the widely referenced paper by Mah et al. (64), sleep extension was demonstrated to improve performance indices ranging from speed, free throw percentage, 3-point field goal percentage and psychomotor vigilance reaction time (PVT) in Division I basketball players.

Sleep management strategies may also play a crucial role in team and individual competition outcomes. Leger et al. (13) examined sleep management and performance during the Tour de France à la Voile 2002 yacht race. Sleep length, sleep debt and sleepiness before and during competition was compared to race performance. Analysis revealed that the final rankings of the race were related to sleep management strategies, with the winner achieving a lower total sleep debt (13). Recently, Juliff et al. (8) found that during a national multiday netball competition, sleep duration was strongly associated with higher final tournament positions (8).

Juliff et al. (8) state that "Sleep is often regarded as the single best recovery strategy available to an athlete". Unfortunately, the literature suggests performance and training adaptation may be compromised due to inadequate sleep in the amateur and professional athlete population, and this problem has not gone unrecognized by athletes themselves (12, 41, 65). According to Lastella et al. (66) "Anecdotal evidence indicates that athletes are concerned about the amount of quality sleep they obtain as they believe that good sleep substantially contributes to their capacity to compete at an optimal level"(66). Therefore, it is imperative that sleep should be considered a critical component of the training process, that impacts both adaptive abilities but also performance outcomes.

Training – An Adaptive Process

On the journey to peak performance, an athlete engages in an integrated systemic process of athlete preparation termed the *training process* (67). According to Smith "The training process involves the repetition of exercises designed to induce automation in the execution of motor skill and develop structural and metabolic functions that lead to increased physical performance" (67). The training process is an adaptation dependent process, as training loads (e.g., physical, psychological) are presented to an athlete's organism with the intent of inducing an adaptive response that improves athlete preparedness. Fomin and Nasedkin (67) define *preparedness* as "The multi-faceted cumulative state of an athlete, composed of a certain developmental level of physical, technical, tactical, mental, and intellectual factors".

In the training process, there is a physiological cost for adaptation associated with any training stimulus (e.g., metabolic, structural, psychological). This *cost of adaptation* (Figure 1), affects an athlete readiness to adapt to subsequent training stimuli. The state of *readiness* is the result of both intrinsic and extrinsic factors, both training and non-training loads (67). For instance, social stress can be a compounding factor in the training process which affects athlete readiness. By considering the state of readiness, the training process can be modified to target specific systems or means of training that can optimize training outcomes. Morris states: "Readiness may be defined as the current functional state of an individual that determines their ability to achieve their performance potential" (68). The functional state of the human organism can be objectively measured by assessing the Direct Current (DC) potential of the brain.

To improve technical or tactical skill, specialized training must occur. All training, whether psychological or physiological, carries a cost of adaptation. For instance, if a football player performs a 2-hour practice session, preceded by weight room session focused on developing strength, a cascade of physiologic processes must occur on the backend to promote recovery and adaptation (e.g., structural, metabolic, neural) to the training stimulus. It is a misnomer to believe that all training sessions result in positive adaptation. If the cost is too high, or the initiation of the training begins in a compromised state of readiness, then the result can be maladaptation, leading to injury or in extreme cases (i.e., exertional rhabdomyolysis), death (refer to Hans Selye's General Adaptation Syndrome).

If motor learning is sequenced appropriately, and adequate restoration is provided between sessions, preparedness (technical-tactical skill) should improve consistently over time (red line in the Figure 1). However, as previously described, to improve technical-tactical skills, training must occur, which carries a cost of adaptation. When peak performance is required, preparedness and readiness must both be in an optimal state. It is possible to be prepared, but not ready. This is when poor performance usually occurs. The training can be on point, but if the body is unable to supply the biological resources to support performance, disaster can occur.

Therefore, the goal in the training process is to develop an adaptable athlete, that recovers quickly from training. This will in turn reduce the cost of adaptation (Figure 1), and enable the athlete to engage in more frequent and intense training, and thus secure more windows for optimal performance.

At this point, I think it's very important to address the elephant in the room. I am about to discuss what most people consider the "black box" of the Omegawave technology. It is often said often that Omegawave doesn't publish the research behind the technology. In fact, it's not their job to publish the research, but rather it's our job to FIND the research. After I conclude writing this chapter for THE MANUAL Vol. 4, I plan to begin the process of publishing a very extensive literature review of DC potential. From a scientific standpoint, it's hard to run from the fact that there is over 70 years of literature documenting its use in the fields of medicine (69, 70, neurophysiology (71), psychophysiology (72) and sports physical preparation (68, 73) for numerous applications. I will "dip my toe" into the literature for THE MANUAL but be on the lookout for a deep dive in the coming months from me.

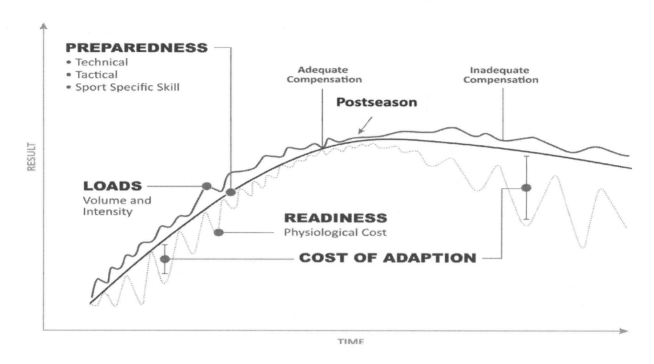

Figure 1. Nasedkin V. & Fomin R. The Concept of Readiness in Managing of the Training Process of Athletes. 2013

Over 80 years ago, H.S. Burr and F.S.C. Northrop wrote "" (74). Burr and Northrop realized that a shift needed to occur in how bioelectric fields were viewed in their relationship to living systems. Their theory stated that the "field determines the behavior of any local process or constituent within it", and this bold statement opened the door for the legitimate examination of measurement tools such as the electroencephalogram (EEG) and the electrocardiogram (EKG). Soon after, pioneers such as Pauline A. Davis began measuring EEG reactions to acoustic sounds using electrodes placed on the scalp, and in 1949 Kohler and Held reported that functional interrelations in the brain where coordinated by a continuous field action which consisted of "direct currents which spread through the brain as a continuum" (75). Kohler and Held found that the behavior of direct currents, measured from the head, agreed with predictions from biophysical theory.

Then along came Natalia Bekhtereva. In 1955, she began recording and analyzing slower wave forms in animals and humans (76,77). Bekhtereva, a Russian neuroscientist and psychologist credited with developing a neurophysiological approach psychology, started recording DC potential using indwelling electrodes in the brains of animals (76).

Bekhtereva would go on to have a distinguished career eventually becoming the Director of the Soviet Institute for Experimental Medicine and the editor-in-chief of academic journals such as "Human Physiology" and the "International Journal of Psychophysiology" (Wiki). In 1972, she was awarded the Wiener medal in cybernetics and went on to be the founder of the Institute of Human Brain.

Bekhtereva's work spawned an explosion in the study of slower wave forms other than the traditionally studied α-waves in humans and animals (76,77). Soon N.A. Aladzhalova and A.V. Kol'tsova identified very slow periodic potentials in the hypothalamus and cerebral cortex, unlike those usually revealed in the electrocorticogram. They named this new frequency "infraslow" (78). These early studies were later supported by numerous physiological studies in which DC potentials were confirmed to represent the slow regulatory system of the brain, which only responds to environmental factors that are intense and frequent in nature (68). Later, Gribanov et al. (79) confirmed this finding and reported that DC potentials are slow changing and one of the most constant physiological processes of the brain. This is important to recognize, because the EEG is used to measure the fast-regulatory systems of the brain that respond to stimuli which are weak or infrequent (68).

In the 1980s, Sychev determined that DC potentials could be measured in a stable millivolt scale using the vertex-tenar (forehead-palm) method which enables the "quick diagnosis of the functional state of athletes, optimization of the training process, and enhances performance in sport" (80). Ilyukhina, a student of Bekhterevas', and Dan'ko developed the specific hardware for multiparametric recording of the functional state, and this became known as the omegametry method for recording DC potential (80). Ilyukhina and Sychev soon outlined quantitative parameters of resting DC potential for assessing adaptation and compensatory adaptabilities to physical and mental loads in sports (80,81). Figure 2 (82) depicts the relationship between DC potential and adaptability in the human organism (Note: This figure was adapted from the work of Dr. Olga Kara).

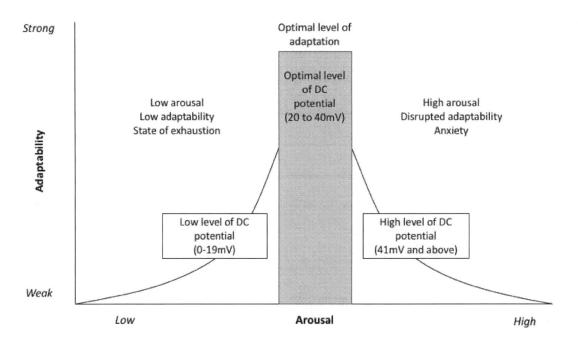

Figure 2.

DC potential has been used in multiple domains outside of sports to examine short and long-term adaptations to stress. Maksimov and Karasi, working as researchers at the Institute of High-Altitude Physiology and Experimental Pathology (in the former USSR), studied the changes in the functional state of engineers that commuted to work in high altitudes. They found that engineers who had been commuting for less than 6 months had significantly higher DC potentials, which "reflect the price the body pays for the process of adaptation in the presence of an increased load on the functional systems of the body" (83).

DC potential has been widely used in medicine to assess the functional state and adaptive systemic reactions of the body in both healthy and diseased states (84). DC potential has been used to study epilepsy (85), hyponotic states (86), emotional disorders (87) and the neurophysiology of intelligence and emotions in humans (88). Krupitsky et al. (89) used DC potential to examine the effects of pharmacological intervention with alcoholic patients with secondary affective disorders (i.e., anxiety and depression). Zhukova studied DC potential changes in pregnant women with endemic goiters (90), and Ilyukhina et al. (91) examined causal factors for dampened compensatory-adaptive reactions of children with subclinical forms of pre- and perinatal CNS pathology.

Finally, and I would highly suggest reading the complete papers in which Vanhatalo et al. (92) and Murik (93) used DC-EEG to examine unique changes in brain states. Vanhatalo et al. studied hemodynamic changes in the human brain, using non-invasive manipulations (e.g., bilateral jugular vein compression, head-down tilt, Valsalva, and Mueller maneuvers) which elicited pressure gradient changes in intracranial compartments. They found that DC potential shifts were consistent and reproducible and demonstrated a "clear temporal correlation with changes in CBV" (92). Murik examined the functional and metabolic state of nervous tissue in the brain during hyper- and hypoventilation states. This was one of the most fascinating papers discovered during my doctoral research, as it clearly demonstrates the use of DC-EEG to study functional and metabolic changes in the nervous tissue of the brain (93). Figure 3, which has been extracted directly from my dissertation, clearly outlines the connection between functional and metabolic changes in nervous tissue and how it impacts DC potential. I recommend the reader to refer back to Figure 2, to clearly see how improved or detrimental metabolic states are accurately reflected in DC potential shifts.

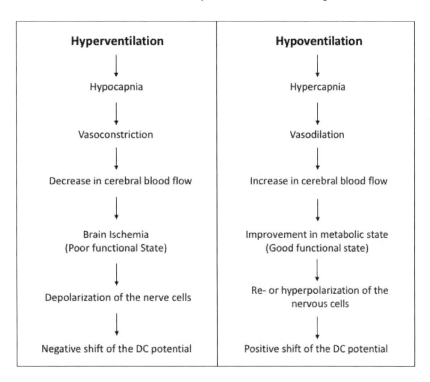

Figure 3. Schematic for the processes occurring in the nervous tissue during hyperventilation and hypoventilation. Adapted from Murik (93)

DC Potential and the Training Process

As I detail in my dissertation, the literature supporting the use of DC potential in the training process is limited because a significant quantity of the research has yet to be translated into English. However, as previously described the literature does support the use of DC potential as an objective measure of short and long-term adaptations to stress (e.g., physiological, psychological, environmental) (94, 95). One of the reasons Sychev developed the vertex-thenar method for the assessment of DC potentials was to assess athletes response to training loads during the training process (81). In the paper, "The Omega-Potential: A Quantitative Parameter of the State of Brain Structures and of the Individual. II. Possibilities and Limitations of the Use of the Omega-Potential for Rapid Assessment of the State of the Individual" Ilyukina et al. (81) detail the responses of various classes of athletes (i.e., Mater of Sport in the International Class in light athletics) to similar loading stimuli using DC potential. The authors also detail investigations in which G.I. Baryshev correlated DC potentials to a combination of 25 psychophysiological parameters in the members of a "Class A" handball team. Barshev determined that there was a significant correlation between resting DC potential values and the results of the psychophysiological tests. It was found that if resting DC potentials were between 20 to 40 mV, subsequently, newly introduced sports skills were acquired and executed at a higher rate (81).

During my time at the University of Kentucky, serving as the High Performance Director for football, Dr. Chris Morris investigated the effects of a fluid periodization model on athletic performance outcomes with our football team (68). Dr. Morris used the Omegawave athlete monitoring system which utilizes a combination of heart rate variability (HRV) and DC potential to assess athlete readiness to train. The treatment group adhered to a fluid periodization model in which volume and intensities of training sessions were modified based upon Omegawave's assessment of athletes' readiness. The control group was not assessed using the Omegwave's AMS and performed a similar training regime as the treatment group that was designed by the Strength and Conditioning staff. Following an 8-week training intervention, the treatment group significantly increased in broad jump (+592%), vertical jump (+157%), lower body vertical power (+94%), and aerobic efficiency (+156%) compared to the unmonitored control group. As a result of using a fluid periodization approach, the treatment group performed 9.5% less arbitrary units of core resistance training volume and 13.2% less volume of accessory exercises. This study indicates that using objective assessments of athlete readiness to guide training results in improvements in athletic performance outcomes concomitant to a reduction in physiological cost to the athlete (68).

Recently, Peterson used machine learning to train numerous predictive models to forecast elite sprint performance (96). Fifteen male Division I NCAA track and field student-athletes who competed in races 200 meters in length or shorter completed the Omegawave assessment (HRV and DC potential) within 24-hours of competition throughout their competitive careers (n = 182). To ensure reliable measurements, the assessment was performed between 0600 and 0800 the morning of the competition. Two opposing quadrants were found to reflect optimal versus sub-optimal performance. Peterson states, "When the athletes recorded higher DC potential accompanied with higher ln-RMSSD, the classifier was more likely to predict optimal athletic performance, and vice versa." The threshold for optimal performance was DC potential above 15mV with ln-RMSSD above 4.25ms. These findings mirror the ranges Ilyukhina et al. (73) devised (Figure 2). In addition, DC potentials < 10mv negatively influenced performance, and optimal values were 25-35mV.

In brief, DC potential has been used in both healthy and diseased populations to assess adaptation and compensatory-adaptive responses to stress (81, 94, 97, 70, 98). The assessment of DC potential, using the vertex-thenar method, allows for the quick and accurate assessment of the functional state of the athlete which can be used in the optimization of the training process (81, 68).

The Connection

Despite the evidence that sleep affects physiological, psychological and performance outcomes, there is a paucity of research that has examined the relationship between sleep and the functional state. I am now taking off my white coat and simply looking that this through a coaching lens, but if sleep affects an athlete's ability to adapt to stress, then this is a very important variable to consider in the training process. It doesn't matter how good the periodization is, or how great I am as a coach: if my athletes aren't in a state in which they can "accept" the training and adapt to in, then our work is in vain.

My doctoral dissertation examined this relationship, and we found that with collegiate American football players, there was a significant relationship between sleep and the functional state (https://uknowledge.uky.edu/khp_etds/52/). My research revealed that acute sleep durations (one night) between 7-9 hours yielded greater DC potential outcomes, compared to sleep of less than 6 hours. In addition, extended sleep periods (two consecutive nights) between 7.5-9 hours yielded greater DC potentials compared to two-night sleep durations averaging less than 6 hours. In addition, my findings revealed that these favorable sleep durations placed the athlete in an optimal state for adaptation, as defined by Ilyukhina et al. (73).

So, what can we distill from all of this? Below are some practical coaching points and my recommendations based on the literature surrounding the impact of sleep and what we know about maximizing the training process.

Coaching Points

1. Sleep quantity is associated with an athlete's function state – READINESS TO TRAIN. If you want to mitigate the risk of minimal or no adaptation to training…make sure your athletes sleep.

2. Optimal Sleep Duration: 7.5 – 9 hours/night

3. If it is important, then measure it. Find a valid, reliable and unobtrusive means to quantify sleep. I highly recommend Fatigue Science. They are affordable for most collegiate and professional sports teams and the feedback is awesome. If you can't afford an objective tool, create a wellness questionnaire using Google sheets and ask your athletes how much they sleep. Most people overestimate their sleep duration by 30min – 1 hour, so factor in that discrepancy.

4. Periods of Restricted Sleep – If your head coach insists on early morning training sessions, or you are constrained because of class schedules etc. then

change in the environment! Stimulate the athletes by using music, games, or your personality. Also, you may need to change the training, by presenting a stimulus to which they may be able to adapt. Protect against the downside and invest in the upside!

5. Basic sleep hygiene

- Your room should be dark and cold…think cave! Less than 70 degrees is optimal.

- Use black-out curtains and if you are in a hotel roll up a towel and place it near the door.

- Stop using devices ~ an hour before bedtime. If you use an iOS device "turn on night shift".

- Blue light blocking glasses are a luxury but work well. Wear them about 60-90 minutes before bed.

6. Get over your ego and look at the literature around Omegawave. We are in the data collection age, and Omegawave is an awesome tool designed to truly understand the cost of training. Use the information to council your athletes and improve your training methodologies.

REFERENCES

1. Hopkins, K. (2005). Facilitating sleep for patients with end stage renal disease. Nephrology Nursing Journal, 32(2).

2. Crocker, A., & Sehgal, A. (2010). Genetic analysis of sleep. Genes & development, 24(12), 1220-1235.

3. Fullagar, H. H., Skorski, S., Duffield, R., Hammes, D., Coutts, A. J., & Meyer, T. (2015). Sleep and athletic performance: the effects of sleep loss on exercise performance, and physiological and cognitive responses to exercise. Sports medicine, 45(2), 161-186.

4. Chien, K. L., Chen, P. C., Hsu, H. C., Su, T. C., Sung, F. C., Chen, M. F., & Lee, Y. T. (2010). Habitual sleep duration and insomnia and the risk of cardiovascular events and all-cause death: report from a community-based cohort. Sleep, 33(2), 177-184.

5. Watson, A. M. (2017). Sleep and athletic performance. Current sports medicine reports, 16(6), 413-418.

6. Shapiro, C. M., Bortz, R., Mitchell, D., Bartel, P., & Jooste, P. (1981). Slow-wave sleep: a recovery period after exercise. Science, 214(4526), 1253-1254.

7. Halson, S. L. (2008). Nutrition, sleep and recovery. European Journal of sport science, 8(2), 119-126.

8. Juliff, L. E., Halson, S. L., Hebert, J. J., Forsyth, P. L., & Peiffer, J. J. (2018). Longer sleep durations are positively associated with finishing place during a national multiday netball competition. The Journal of Strength & Conditioning Research, 32(1), 189-194.

9. Arnal, P. J., Lapole, T., Erblang, M., Guillard, M., Bourrilhon, C., Leger, D., ... & Millet, G. Y. (2016). Sleep extension before sleep loss: effects on

performance and neuromuscular function. Med Sci Sports Exerc, 48(8), 1595-1603.

10. Azboy, O., & Kaygisiz, Z. (2009). Effects of sleep deprivation on cardiorespiratory functions of the runners and volleyball players during rest and exercise. Acta Physiologica Hungarica, 96(1), 29-36.

11. Bulbulian, R., Heaney, J. H., Leake, C. N., Sucec, A. A., & Sjoholm, N. T. (1996). The effect of sleep deprivation and exercise load on isokinetic leg strength and endurance. European journal of applied physiology and occupational physiology, 73(3-4), 273-277.

12. Gupta, L., Morgan, K., & Gilchrist, S. (2017). Does elite sport degrade sleep quality? A systematic review. Sports Medicine, 47(7), 1317-1333.

13. Leger, D., Elbaz, M., Raffray, T., Metlaine, A., Bayon, V., & Duforez, F. (2008). Sleep management and the performance of eight sailors in the Tour de France a la voile yacht race. Journal of sports sciences, 26(1), 21-28.

14. Reilly, T., & Piercy, M. (1994). The effect of partial sleep deprivation on weight-lifting performance. Ergonomics, 37(1), 107-115.

15. Skein, M., Duffield, R., Edge, J., Short, M. J., & Muendel, T. (2011). Intermittent-sprint performance and muscle glycogen after 30 h of sleep deprivation. Medicine & Science in Sports & Exercise, 43(7), 1301-1311.

16. Thomas, V., & Reilly, T. (1975). Circulatory, psychological & performance variables during 100 hours of paced continuous exercise under conditions of controlled energy intake & work output. Journal of Human Movement Studies.

17. Samuels, C., James, L., Lawson, D., & Meeuwisse, W. (2016). The Athlete Sleep Screening Questionnaire: a new tool for assessing and managing sleep in elite athletes. Br J Sports Med, 50(7), 418-422.

18. Stickgold, R. (2005). Sleep-dependent memory consolidation. Nature, 437(7063), 1272.

19. Allada, R., & Siegel, J. M. (2008). Unearthing the phylogenetic roots of sleep. Current biology, 18(15), R670-R679.

20. Nikhil, K. L., & Sharma, V. K. (2013). Circadian rhythms. Resonance, 18(9), 832-844.

21. Somers, V., Javaheri, S., Kryger, M., Roth, T., & Dement, W. C. (2017). Principles and practices of sleep medicine.

22. Thun, E., Bjorvatn, B., Flo, E., Harris, A., & Pallesen, S. (2015). Sleep, circadian rhythms, and athletic performance. Sleep medicine reviews, 23, 1-9.

23. Refinetti, R., & Menaker, M. (1992). The circadian rhythm of body temperature. Physiology & behavior, 51(3), 613-637.

24. Beersma, D. G., & Gordijn, M. C. (2007). Circadian control of the sleep–wake cycle. Physiology & behavior, 90(2-3), 190-195.

25. McCormick, F., Kadzielski, J., Landrigan, C. P., Evans, B., Herndon, J. H., & Rubash, H. E. (2012). Surgeon fatigue: a prospective analysis of the incidence, risk, and intervals of predicted fatigue-related impairment in residents. Archives of Surgery, 147(5), 430-435.

26. Stephan FK and Zucker I. Circadian rhythms in drinking behavior and locomotor activity of rats are eliminated by hypothalamic lesions. Proceedings of the National Academy of Sciences 69: 1583-1586, 1972.

27. Borbély, A. A. (1982). A two-process model of sleep regulation. Hum neurobiol, 1(3), 195-204.

28. Van Dongen, H., Maislin, G., Mullington, J. M., & Dinges, D. F. (2003). The cumulative cost of additional wakefulness: dose-response effects on neurobehavioral functions and sleep physiology from chronic sleep restriction and total sleep deprivation. Sleep, 26(2), 117-126.

29. Drust, B., Waterhouse, J., Atkinson, G., Edwards, B., & Reilly, T. (2005). Circadian rhythms in sports performance—an update. Chronobiology international, 22(1), 21-44.

30. Borb, A. A., & Achermann, P. (1999). Sleep homeostasis and models of sleep regulation. Journal of biological rhythms, 14(6), 559-570.

31. Carskadon, M. A., & Dement, W. C. (2005). Normal human sleep: an overview. Principles and practice of sleep medicine, 4, 13-23.

32. Schupp, M., & Hanning, C. D. (2003). Physiology of sleep. Bja Cepd Reviews, 3(3), 69-74.

33. Morris, C. J., Aeschbach, D., & Scheer, F. A. (2012). Circadian system, sleep and endocrinology. Molecular and cellular endocrinology, 349(1), 91-104.

34. Gronfier, C., Luthringer, R., Follenius, M., Schaltenbrand, N., Macher, J. P., Muzet, A., & Brandenberger, G. (1996). A quantitative evaluation of the relationships between growth hormone secretion and delta wave electroencephalographic activity during normal sleep and after enrichment in delta waves. Sleep, 19(10), 817-824.

35. Isaksson, O. G., Jansson, J. O., & Gause, I. A. (1982). Growth hormone stimulates longitudinal bone growth directly. Science, 216(4551), 1237-1239.

36. Cuneo, R. C., Salomon, F. R. A. N. C., Wiles, C. M., Hesp, R., & Sonksen, P. H. (1991). Growth hormone treatment in growth hormone-deficient adults. I. Effects on muscle mass and strength. Journal of Applied Physiology, 70(2), 688-694.

37. Chien, K. L., Chen, P. C., Hsu, H. C., Su, T. C., Sung, F. C., Chen, M. F., & Lee, Y. T. (2010). Habitual sleep duration and insomnia and the risk of cardiovascular events and all-cause death: report from a community-based cohort. Sleep, 33(2), 177-184.

38. Siegel, J. M. (2005). Clues to the functions of mammalian sleep. Nature, 437(7063), 1264.

39. Watson, N. F., Buchwald, D., Delrow, J. J., Altemeier, W. A., Vitiello, M. V., Pack, A. I., ... & Gharib, S. A. (2017). Transcriptional signatures of sleep duration discordance in monozygotic twins. Sleep, 40(1).

40. Spiegel, K., Leproult, R., & Van Cauter, E. (1999). Impact of sleep debt on metabolic and endocrine function. The lancet, 354(9188), 1435-1439.

41. Gapstur SM. Shorter sleep duration is associated with increased risk of fatal prostate cancer in younger men. Presented at American Association for Cancer Research, Wahsington, DC, 2017.

42. Erren, T. C., Falaturi, P., Morfeld, P., Knauth, P., Reiter, R. J., & Piekarski, C. (2010). Shift work and cancer: the evidence and the challenge. Deutsches Ärzteblatt International, 107(38), 657.

43. Shan, Z., Ma, H., Xie, M., Yan, P., Guo, Y., Bao, W., ... & Liu, L. (2015). Sleep duration and risk of type 2 diabetes: a meta-analysis of prospective studies. Diabetes care, 38(3), 529-537.

44. Potter, G. D., Cade, J. E., & Hardie, L. J. (2017). Longer sleep is associated with lower BMI and favorable metabolic profiles in UK adults: Findings from the National Diet and Nutrition Survey. PloS one, 12(7), e0182195.

45. Walker, M. P., Stickgold, R., Alsop, D., Gaab, N., & Schlaug, G. (2005). Sleep-dependent motor memory plasticity in the human brain. Neuroscience, 133(4), 911-917.

46. Benington, J. H., & Frank, M. G. (2003). Cellular and molecular connections between sleep and synaptic plasticity. Progress in neurobiology, 69(2), 71-101.

47. De Vivo, L., Bellesi, M., Marshall, W., Bushong, E. A., Ellisman, M. H., Tononi, G., & Cirelli, C. (2017). Ultrastructural evidence for synaptic scaling across the wake/sleep cycle. Science, 355(6324), 507-510.

48. Spencer, R. M., Walker, M. P., & Stickgold, R. (2017). Sleep and memory consolidation. In Sleep Disorders Medicine (pp. 205-223). Springer, New York, NY.

49. Frank, M. G., & Benington, J. H. (2006). The role of sleep in memory consolidation and brain plasticity: dream or reality?. The Neuroscientist, 12(6), 477-488.

50. Tononi G and Cirelli C. Sleep and the price of plasticity: from synaptic and cellular homeostasis to memory consolidation and integration. Neuron 81: 12-34, 2014.

51. Wang, Z., Ma, J., Miyoshi, C., Li, Y., Sato, M., Ogawa, Y., ... & Fujiyama, T. (2018). Quantitative phosphoproteomic analysis of the molecular substrates of sleep need. Nature, 558(7710), 435.

52. Bompa, T., & Haff, G. G. (2009). Periodization: Theory and Methodology of Training.: Human kinetics. ISBN-13, 978-0736074834.

53. Mah, C. D., Kezirian, E. J., Marcello, B. M., & Dement, W. C. (2018). Poor sleep quality and insufficient sleep of a collegiate student-athlete population. Sleep health, 4(3), 251-257.

54. Simpson, N. S., Gibbs, E. L., & Matheson, G. O. (2017). Optimizing sleep to maximize performance: implications and recommendations for elite athletes. Scandinavian journal of medicine & science in sports, 27(3), 266-274.

55. Oliver, S. J., Costa, R. J., Laing, S. J., Bilzon, J. L., & Walsh, N. P. (2009). One night of sleep deprivation decreases treadmill endurance performance. European journal of applied physiology, 107(2), 155-161.

56. Goel N, Rao H, Durmer JS, and Dinges DF. Neurocognitive consequences of sleep deprivation. Presented at Seminars in Neurology, 2009

57. Skein, M., Duffield, R., Edge, J., Short, M. J., & Muendel, T. (2011). Intermittent-sprint performance and muscle glycogen after 30 h of sleep deprivation. Medicine & Science in Sports & Exercise, 43(7), 1301-1311.

58. Takeuchi, L., Davis, G. M., Plyley, M., Goode, R., & Shephard, R. J. (1985). Sleep deprivation, chronic exercise and muscular performance. Ergonomics, 28(3), 591-601.

59. Blumert PA, Crum AJ, Ernsting M, Volek JS, Hollander DB, Haff EE, and Haff GG. The acute effects of twenty-four horus of sleep loss on the performance of national caliber male collegiate weightlifters. The Journal of Strength & Conditioning Research 21: 1146-1154, 2007.

60. Sinnerton S and Reilly T. Effects of sleep loss and time of day in swimmers. Biomechanics and medicine in swimming: swimming science IV London: E and FN Spon: 399-405, 1992.

61. Edwards, B. J., & Waterhouse, J. (2009). Effects of one night of partial sleep deprivation upon diurnal rhythms of accuracy and consistency in throwing darts. Chronobiology international, 26(4), 756-768.

62. Reyner, L. A., & Horne, J. A. (2013). Sleep restriction and serving accuracy in performance tennis players, and effects of caffeine. Physiology & behavior, 120, 93-96.

63. Schwartz, J., & Simon Jr, R. D. (2015). Sleep extension improves serving accuracy: A study with college varsity tennis players. Physiology & behavior, 151, 541-544.

64. Mah, C. D., Mah, K. E., Kezirian, E. J., & Dement, W. C. (2011). The effects of sleep extension on the athletic performance of collegiate basketball players. Sleep, 34(7), 943-950.

65. Shearer, D. A., Jones, R. M., Kilduff, L. P., & Cook, C. J. (2015). Effects of competition on the sleep patterns of elite rugby union players. European journal of sport science, 15(8), 681-686.

66. Lastella, M., Roach, G. D., Halson, S. L., & Sargent, C. (2015). Sleep/wake behaviours of elite athletes from individual and team sports. European Journal of Sport Science, 15(2), 94-100.

67. Fomin, R., & Nasedkin, V. (2013). EFFECTIVE MANAGEMENT OF ATHLETE PREPARATION.

68. Morris, C. W. (2015). The effect of fluid periodization on athletic performance outcomes in American football players.

69. Ilyuchina, V. A., & Nikitina, L. I. (1995). Clinical physiological study of the therapeutic effects of phenytoin in acute alcohol withdrawal and the asthenic-autonomic syndrome in patients with chronic alcoholism. Alcohol, 12(6), 511-517.

70. Krupitsky E, Burakov A, Ivanov V, Krandashova G, Lapin I, Grinenko AJ, and Borodkin YS. Baclofen administration for the treatment of affective disorders in alcoholic patients. Drug & Alcohol Dependence 33: 157-163, 1993.

71. Bechtyereva, N. P., Bundzen, P. V., Gogolitsyn, Y. L., & Medvedev, S. V. (1981). PHYSIOLOGICAL CORRELATES OF STATES AND ACTIVITIES IN THE CENTRAL NERVOUS SYSTEM. In Brain and Behaviour (pp. 395-404). Pergamon.

72. Starchenko, M. G., Bechtereva, N. P., Tamatorin, I. V., Sazhin, V. L., & Dobrovol'skii, S. I. (2003). On the Possibility of Correcting Emotional Disorders under the Conditions of the Action of a Destabilizing Factor. Human Physiology, 29(4), 486-491.

73. Ilyukhina, V. A., Sychev, A. G., Shcherbakova, N. I., Baryshev, G. I., & Denisova, V. V. (1982). The omega-potential: A quantitative parameter of the state of brain structures and of the individual: II. Possibilities and limitations of the use of the omega-potential for rapid assessment of the state of the individual. Human physiology.

74. Burr, H. S., & Northrop, F. S. C. (1935). The electro-dynamic theory of life. The Quarterly Review of Biology, 10(3), 322-333.

75. Köhler, W., & Held, R. (1949). The cortical correlate of pattern vision. Science, 110(2860), 414-419.

76. Bekhtereva, N. P., & Danovich, F. M. (1956). The origin of slow rhythmic potentials in the electroencephalogram of rabbits. Bulletin of Experimental Biology and Medicine, 41(2), 95-98.

77. Bekhtereva, N. P. (1957). Some possible forms of intensification of slow waves in the electroencephalogram. Bulletin of Experimental Biology and Medicine, 44, 114-117.

78. Aladzhalova, N. A., & Kol'tsova, A. V. (1958). Very slow rhythmic variations in the potential of the nuclei of the hypothalamus and the thalamus. Bulletin of Experimental Biology and Medicine, 46(4), 1153-1157.

79. Gribanov A, Pankov M, and Podoplekin A. The level of cerebral DC potentials in children with attention deficit-hyperactivity disorder. Human physiology 35: 690-695, 2009

80. Ilyukhina, V. A. (2013). Ultraslow information control systems in the integration of life activity processes in the brain and body. Human physiology, 39(3), 323-333.

81. Ilyukhina, V. A., Sychev, A. G., Shcherbakova, N. I., Baryshev, G. I., & Denisova, V. V. (1982). The omega-potential: A quantitative parameter of the state of brain structures and of the individual: II. Possibilities and limitations of the use of the omega-potential for rapid assessment of the state of the individual. Human physiology.

82. Kara O. Validation of Omegawave's Technology for Assessing Infra Slow Brain Activity (DC Potential). Brain Fitness, 2017

83. Maksimov, A. L., & Karasj, M. F. (1989). Changes in the omega-potential as prognostic criteria of the functional status of the body. International Journal of Psychophysiology, 7(2-4), 301-302.

84. Iliukhina, V. A., Tkachev, V. V., Fedorov, B. M., Reushkina, G. D., & Sebekina, T. V. (1989). Omega-potential measurement in studying the

functional status of healthy subjects with normal and hypertensive types of reaction to graded physical exertion. Fiziologiia cheloveka, 15(2), 60.

85. Bechtyereva, N. P., Bundzen, P. V., Gogolitsyn, Y. L., & Medvedev, S. V. (1981). PHYSIOLOGICAL CORRELATES OF STATES AND ACTIVITIES IN THE CENTRAL NERVOUS SYSTEM. In Brain and Behaviour (pp. 395-404). Pergamon.

86. Aladzhalova N, Rozhnov V, and Kamenetskii S. Hypnosis in man and very slow brain electrical activity. Neuroscience and Behavioral Physiology 9: 252-256, 1978

87. Starchenko, M. G., Bechtereva, N. P., Tamatorin, I. V., Sazhin, V. L., & Dobrovol'skii, S. I. (2003). On the Possibility of Correcting Emotional Disorders under the Conditions of the Action of a Destabilizing Factor. Human Physiology, 29(4), 486-491.

88. Bechtereva N. Neurophysiology of intellectual and emotional processes in man. International Journal of Psychophysiology 1: 7-12, 1983

89. Krupitsky, E. M., Burakov, A. M., Ivanov, V. B., Krandashova, G. F., Lapin, I. P., Grinenko, A. J., & Borodkin, Y. S. (1993). Baclofen administration for the treatment of affective disorders in alcoholic patients. Drug and alcohol dependence, 33(2), 157-163.

90. Zhukova, T. P. (2005). Omegametry in examination of pregnant women with endemic goiter. Human Physiology, 31(4), 445-448.

91. Ilyukhina V, Kozhushko NY, Matveev YK, and Shaitor V. Main Factors of a Decrease in Stress Resistance in Six-to Eight-Year-Old Children with Long-Term Consequences of Perinatal CNS Pathology during Transition to School Period of Their Activity. Human Physiology 28: 253-262, 2002.

92. Vanhatalo, S., Tallgren, P., Becker, C., Holmes, M. D., Miller, J. W., Kaila, K., & Voipio, J. (2003). Scalp-recorded slow EEG responses generated in response

to hemodynamic changes in the human brain. Clinical Neurophysiology, 114(9), 1744-1754.

93. Murik, S. (2012). The use of DCEEG to estimate functional and metabolic state of nervous tissue of the brain at hyper-and hypoventilation. World Journal of Neuroscience, 2(03), 172.

94. Ilyukhina, V. A., & Zabolotskikh, I. B. (2000). Physiological basis of differences in the body tolerance to submaximal physical load to capacity in healthy young individuals. Human physiology, 26(3), 330-336.

95. Maksimov, A. L., & Karasj, M. F. (1989). Changes in the omega-potential as prognostic criteria of the functional status of the body. International Journal of Psychophysiology, 7(2-4), 301-302.

96. Peterson, K. D. (2018). Resting Heart Rate Variability Can Predict Track and Field Sprint Performance. OA Journal-Sports, 1(1).

97. Maksimov, A. L., & Karasj, M. F. (1989). Changes in the omega-potential as prognostic criteria of the functional status of the body. International Journal of Psychophysiology, 7(2-4), 301-302.

98. O'Leary, J. L., & Goldring, S. (1964). DC potentials of the brain. Physiological reviews, 44(1), 91-125.

Who is Dr. Erik Korem?

Dr. Erik Korem is a national and cross-border operations executive with longstanding experience overseeing the design implementation of high-performance programming for professional and collegiate athletics. Erik has contributed to full cycle selection and development processes in the collegiate (Florida State University, University of Kentucky, Mississippi State University) and professional football (Houston Texans). Erik currently serves as the Associate Athletics Director of Student-Athlete High Performance at William and Mary where he manages and leads a cross-functional team across sports medicine, health and performance psychology, and athletics performance. Erik is a former Division I athlete and a lifelong learner holding a BS in Applied Exercise Physiology from Texas A&M University, MS in Exercise Science from the University of Arkansas, and a PhD in Exercise Science from the University of Kentucky.

Made in the USA
Middletown, DE
06 July 2019